Into the Hands of Leaders

Into the Hands of Leaders

Employee Growth through Learning

● ●

Hannah Brown, M. Ed.

hannahbrown
LEAD WITH LEARNING

First published in 2024 by Hambone Publishing
Melbourne, Australia

Editing by Mish Phillips, Laura McCall and Emily Stephenson
Cover design by Brett Lamb
Interior design by David W. Edelstein

For information about this title, contact:
Hannah Brown
hannah@hannahbrown.co
www.hannahbrown.co

ISBN 978-1-922357-83-0 (paperback)
ISBN 978-1-922357-84-7 (eBook)
ISBN 978-1-922357-73-1 (audiobook)

To my children.

*Jack, may you always be curious
about the world around you.*

*Olivia, may you continue to find the courage
to boldly step into new situations.*

Preface

We need a different approach to employee development – one that is appropriate to our current times. We need employees to fully engage and participate, knowing it will be worthwhile and will help them grow in their jobs. We cannot risk employees not learning and growing. We cannot rely on formal training alone to develop our people.

In the summer of 2023, I had lunch with Laura[i], a client who manages a Learning and Development (L&D) department at a national insurance company. As our conversation unfolded, she shared how her team created a Change Management program for their leaders. The program focused on how people respond differently to change and how leaders can support their teams. After the program, Laura asked the leaders what support they needed to implement what they had learned. The leaders responded with several ideas and topics for future training.

(i)   Name has been changed to maintain anonymity.

> *The L&D team followed up with a multidimensional*
> *workshop on resiliency. The short workshop referenced*
> *TED Talks and online resources and had an MS Teams*
> *Channel for informal discussion and learning. When they*
> *launched this follow-up workshop, only half a dozen of the*
> *organization's 100+ leaders attended.*

From a learning and development perspective, this is an experience I've heard repeatedly over my decades working in the field. It may sound a bit different – "Training doesn't stick," "Poor uptake," or "Difficulty measuring training impact" – but it's the same message. Learning isn't targeted nor evaluated for return on the investment and it doesn't change behaviour. L&D professionals like my client Laura are frustrated with the lacklustre response to programs they work hard to create.

From an employee's perspective, formal training programs are too generic. They are not targeted to their specific needs and don't consider their previous knowledge and experience of the topic. Courses include more information than is necessary, and content is either too basic or too advanced. Employees express this as, "Training takes too long, and I can't apply it."

From an organization or senior leader's perspective, there is little to no accountability for training impact. Vanity metrics such as the number of sessions offered, number of employees trained, and employee satisfaction provide no meaningful data on training effectiveness. It's no wonder training is such an easy budget to cut when times are tough. It's not uncommon to hear of a Human Resources department having their budget cut by 30% with no warning and no apparent reason.

How do we ensure our employees learn and grow?

When I think of a more holistic approach to employee growth and development, I picture a partially constructed bridge. The bridge represents growth through learning – for individuals, teams and organizations. Perhaps a leader wants their team to be more innovative, or an organization wants to be more resilient and adaptable to change. Perhaps employees are disengaging and turnover is increasing. The bridge represents engaged employees who are expanding their skills, a high-performing team that innovates, and a resilient organization positioned for the future.

One side of the bridge, let's say the left side, represents the Learning and Development department. Just as my client, Laura, had described at lunch, this department is responsible for formal training programs like change management and resiliency training. Even when these programs are well designed, specific to the audience, and provide targeted information, they only get us part way. We need the other side of the bridge: learning and growth at the individual and team levels. This right side is focused not on a learning department but on learning that is embedded in the DNA of the organization. We know, and research[1] confirms, that most learning happens on the job – in conversation and working with colleagues. We also know that teams play a crucial role in highly effective organizations. Teams perform better than individuals[2] and are a defining component of an organization's competitive advantage. From a learning perspective, when teams share knowledge across departments, the knowledge contributes to organizational performance.[3] Leaders have a tremendous role in shaping their team culture and can amplify the learning that occurs naturally. The challenge is that leaders often feel ill-equipped to support their employees' development. Some hesitate because they lack confidence in their ability to have coaching or career conversations. Others are unsure of their organization's policies and are afraid of misstepping when coaching. They are concerned that they'll commit to a course of action that isn't possible within the organization's parameters. Finally, almost all leaders I work with are starved for time. Even when they know coaching and developing their employees is an important part of their role as a leader, they struggle to make time to do so.

In my analogy of the partially constructed bridge, when the formal training programs created by Learning and Development meet leaders who actively coach and develop their employees, the gap in the bridge is narrowed and even closed. Organizations grow when their people grow.

This book is about the right side of the bridge – why we need to invest in our leaders and their teams and focus on growth through learning. Leaders need to take an active role in coaching and developing their employees. Yes, leaders lack time and frequently struggle to manage competing priorities. They are often overworked and, like their employees, suffering burnout from constant change. And yet, when leaders play the long game and invest in their people through coaching and developing their skills, everyone benefits.

The stakes are high. Organizations need to be more resilient, and leaders and employees struggle under the weight of constant change. To survive and thrive, we need to adapt – as individuals and as organizations. As Charles Darwin famously said,

*"It is not the strongest of the species that survives,
nor the most intelligent that survives. It is the one
that is the most adaptable to change."*

I have deep expertise in adult education and learning design. This book is about why learning and development in the traditional sense is not enough; we invest too much in a broken system. When employee growth and learning are confined to a department whose formal training programs don't help employees, teams, or organizations adapt and grow, we need to shift our focus. We need to embed growth through learning into the DNA of our teams. Only then will our partially constructed bridges become expressways for new skills, development, and innovation.

Hannah

Who Is This Book For?

I've written this book for leaders who agree that organizations grow when their people grow. You know your team and organization need to be resilient and adapt to manage constant change and disruption. You recognize that employees are your organization's competitive advantage and are open to new ways of engaging them and developing their skills.

- You may be an executive of a medium-sized, growing company and intuitively know the importance of developing your people. However, given your smaller budgets and flat structure, which offers fewer promotional opportunities, you struggle to do so effectively.
- You may lead a team of people and want them to be more engaged, have a purpose behind their work and develop new capabilities. You know that when your team is engaged, they can do great things.
- You may be a leader in Human Resources or Learning and Development and responsible for employee development across your organization. Like Laura in the Preface, you are frustrated with low adoption and

lack of support for your programs. You understand the limitations of formal training and are looking for a way to move learning out of the sole domain of the department so there is a collective responsibility for employee development across your organization.

Regardless of the size of your organization or whether you are officially responsible for employee learning and development, you are a leader and have an important role in employee learning and growth. You want to help your organization grow and be prepared for the challenges and opportunities that await.

How to Use This Book

A Growth through Learning orientation is the imperative of our time. As you'll read in Chapter One, our shrinking labour pool and the new skill sets that are required make hiring and retaining a top workforce an ongoing challenge. Our volatile, uncertain, complex, and ambiguous (VUCA) environment requires resiliency and adaptability for individuals, teams and organizations.

This book is organized around the Growth through Learning model in Chapter Three. The sections are:

- **A focus on output**
  Describes this approach, including how leaders operate and the experience for employees.
- **A focus on learning**
  Outlines the transition from output to growth and how leaders can embrace or resist learning for themselves and their teams.
- **A focus on growth**
  Provides an alternative to an output culture. Here, leaders prioritize learning alongside results and achieving long-term sustained growth.

I interviewed 20 leaders as I researched this book to confirm the need for a new approach to employee learning and development. Our conversations informed the Growth through Learning model in Chapter Three and the structure of the book. You'll find their stories throughout – either anonymously or with attribution. Many of the leaders I talked with graciously agreed to record our conversation and share the recording publicly. I have created a six-episode podcast, *Growth through Learning: Leadership Conversations for Employee Development*, where you can hear directly from leaders in Human Resources, Learning and Development and functional leaders who manage teams.

To hear from the leaders in my *Growth through Learning* podcast, go to **www.hannahbrown.co/resources/podcast** or wherever you find your podcasts.

Contents

A Focus on Growth

Conclusion

Introduction

"An organization's ability to learn, and translate that learning into action rapidly, is the ultimate competitive advantage."

— Jack Welch

CHAPTER 1
Challenges We Face

L abour shortages, supply chain disruptions, social polarization, unrest, and war. The list could easily go on. We are facing a myriad of challenges. Many describe this as VUCA (volatile, uncertain, complex, and ambiguous), and it's become shorthand for the complicated situations in which we live, work, and learn. For over ten years, I have facilitated a business leadership program for Linamar Corporation, a global automotive parts manufacturer. The executive leadership team was instrumental in the program's original design in 2012 and has been incredibly active in each of the cohorts over the years. Linda Hasenfratz, the executive chair of the board, opens each workshop on the first morning. This past year, she spoke about many of these challenges and added that some business fundamentals like globalization and truth of information are also being challenged in today's political economy.

I want to focus on four challenges affecting our organizations to set the stage for why we need to focus on growth through learning and put employee learning and development into the hands of leaders instead of relying on formal training.

1. Talent and employee skill shortages
2. Need for better employee engagement
3. Rapid technological change
4. Need for organizations to be resilient and adaptable.

1. Talent and employee skill shortages

"The competition to hire the best will increase in the years ahead. Companies that give extra flexibility to their employees will have the edge in this area."

\- Bill Gates, Founder of Microsoft Corporation

Our demographics are permanently changing, which is leaving organizations scrambling to hire and retain the employees they need. This is a global phenomenon, which means organizations can't hire their way out of the challenge but need to grow and develop their existing people.

Global population growth peaked in the 1960s,[4] and since the 1970s, experts identified overpopulation and overconsumption as a global challenge. Governments and people responded. Fast forward to today, and we now face a declining population growth rate and an aging population across the globe. After completing my undergraduate degree, I started working in the employment and talent industry. I heard about the Baby Boomers' looming retirement and its impact on our organizations. It's no longer looming – we're in the middle of it. Statistics Canada has recorded that more than 1 in 5 people is close to retirement, representing an all-time high in the history of the

Canadian census.[5] At a time when people are retiring in droves, we're unable to fill positions because of a smaller pool of labour. This declining population growth rate has implications for our organizations' ability to grow and succeed. When we all compete for a smaller pool of workers, we need to be creative in how we attract people and how we retain a skilled workforce.

It is not enough for organizations to hire their way to a capable workforce. In addition to strong recruitment efforts, organizations must focus on developing their employees. In a tight labour market, there's a greater need to develop talent internally. In the DDI Global Leadership Forecast, 33% of respondents said there will be a significant increase in the need to develop internal talent.[6]

Against this global backdrop of an aging population and a shrinking workforce, there are additional factors contributing to leaders' struggles in hiring the best and brightest for their teams.

Contributing factors: Skills, values, and leaders

The challenge of recruiting and retaining a talented workforce isn't just a story of demographics. There are three additional factors that contribute to this overarching challenge.

NEW SKILLS NEEDED

I can't think of one industry that hasn't been affected by technology and digitization. My family roots are in farming, which has become so sophisticated that weeding fields can be done with AI-driven machines that identify weeds and laser them to stop their growth.[7] Imagine the different skill sets the farmer needs to hire to manage her farm. Instead of general farm labourers, she needs a specially trained technician who can program and operate the autonomous laser weeder.

The fear, of course, is that AI and technology will replace our jobs. I read a post on LinkedIn entitled "How close is AI to replacing instructional designers?"[8] I think the title is misleading. The more correct frame is, "How will AI disrupt and change instructional design?" From a place of fear, technology can make us redundant. From a place of curiosity and abundance, it can make our work easier and more interesting.

I attended a panel discussion at the University of Waterloo on *The Impact of AI on the Future of Work.*[9] The panellists said AI would automate routine, repetitive tasks, allowing employees to focus on higher-order cognitive skills, such as creativity, analysis and evaluation. Hiring and developing employees will focus more on skill sets than pre-defined roles. For example, instead of hiring a 'prompt engineer,' leaders will focus on hiring an employee with 'prompt engineering skills.'

Research, trade magazines, and social media all highlight the skills shortages. It's estimated that by 2030, demand for skilled workers will outstrip supply, resulting in a global talent shortage of more than 85.2 million people.[10] Put another way, 45% of organizations have current skill gaps and anticipate that the gaps will continue into the next five years.[11] Many organizations are responding with increased investment in learning and development. Walmart is investing $1 billion into reskilling its workforce. McDonald's has spent $165 million over the past eight years to prepare its employees. The Association for Talent Development estimates that organizations spend almost $1,300 per employee on professional learning.[12]

Part of the challenge is that technology is changing so fast.

We know that our workplaces will change, and employees will need skills to work alongside technology. But we can't fully anticipate in what ways. I have two teenage children, and as they approach high school graduation and consider continuing education and careers, I'm keenly aware that they will study and work in careers that may not exist yet. Leaders need to hire and develop people for skills and roles that haven't been defined.

EMPLOYEE VALUES AND PRIORITIES

Another contributing factor to the talent shortage is how the COVID-19 pandemic caused people to reconsider their values, question how they spend their time, and scrutinize the environments in which they work. At the same time as this re-evaluation, the pandemic forced organizations to move their workforce to remote work, which provided employees with far greater job opportunities than they previously had access to.

> *Christy Billan is the director of Small Business Lending Products at Farm Credit Canada (FCC). She shared that finding and recruiting talent is one of the top challenges for leaders and organizations and has become increasingly difficult over the past couple of years. She identified the pandemic's impact on opening up a world of remote work as a contributing factor. Employees have more choices as a result and increased power about where and how they want to work.*

To understand why employees leave their jobs, we can look at two variables that influence their decision.[13] The first is the trigger, which comes from the organization or the environment.

Examples of organization triggers include a lack of recognition ("My company doesn't recognize my efforts"), and a lack of flexibility ("My organization doesn't give me a lot of autonomy over how I work"). Triggers can also come from the external environment and include competitive pay ("Another organization would pay me 15% more for doing the same job") and personal growth ("I want to go back to school") The other variable is the employee's motivation, which can be personal or work-related. In the above examples, lack of recognition and competitive pay are work-related, and autonomy and returning to school are personal.

Understanding the triggers and motivation can help leaders focus on where they can have the greatest impact on their employees' decision to stay or leave. For example, if an employee decides to leave because they want to go back to school, the trigger is external, and the motivation is personal. There is little the manager can do to influence the employee's decision. Their best response is to support their employee and maintain a positive relationship. However, if an employee wants to leave because of lack of recognition, the trigger comes from the organization and the motivation is work-related. Here, the leader has a tremendous opportunity to influence the decision. In a tight labour market, it behooves the leader to take action, try to remedy the situation, and retain the employee. As leaders, we need to identify what situations we can influence and where we can focus our efforts to retain our top people.

It feels like the tectonic plates of our workplaces have shifted with the COVID-19 pandemic, and employees' triggers and motivators have changed.

Adam Stephens is the director of Marketing and Community Engagement at The Humane Society of Kitchener Waterloo & Stratford Perth. Adam started his career in marketing for the arts and social services. He described being blessed with many mentors who helped shape his career and his transition into leadership. Adam talked about the books he read, the support he received from his coach, and even insights he gained from the Netflix series 'Ted Lasso.'

Adam's approach to leading his team is beautiful and centred on empathy. He role models vulnerability and talks about "going to bat" for his team members if they're struggling. He also recognizes his limitations and the benefit of being complemented by talented team members.

We talked about the changing relationship between employers and employees. Historically, employees worked their entire careers for one organization. In return, the company provided income, benefits, and a retirement fund. In the 1980s, there was a significant change in this relationship. Organizations laid off employees and eliminated pensions. This started a shift towards more contract workers, which has continued and given rise to the 'gig economy.'[14] Recognizing the importance of employee retention, managers like Adam are now trying to create more ideal workplaces so employees are encouraged to stay and contribute to the success of their team and organization today and in the future.

To expand on my conversation with Adam, the 1980s saw the beginnings of digital transformation as the internet permeated our personal lives and workplaces. The 2008 global economic crash caused mass unemployment and led the way for organizations to replace salaried workers with contract workers. These changes placed more power with organizations and less with employees. The COVID-19 pandemic represented a significant shift and swung the pendulum in the other direction by increasing the power for employees. Employees questioned their work; what they did, who they worked for, and why. They questioned if their work was of value to them. Employees want to have a sense of purpose in their work and to feel fulfilled.[15] If their job didn't provide it, employees felt free to leave for something different. The pandemic helped employees find their voice and gave them the courage to look for other opportunities and move if they found something more desirable. Working remotely opened up new opportunities. People were no longer bound by geography, so they could take their new passions, interests, and purpose-driven desire for work and demand a better work environment. In July 2021, four million Americans left their jobs – that's in one month![16]

Listen to my conversation with Adam in my *Growth through Learning* podcast. Go to **www.hannahbrown.co/resources/podcast** or wherever you find your podcasts.

While an organization's mission, culture, and policies lay the foundation, an employee's experience at work is directly impacted by the manager. Leaders are on the front lines recruiting skilled employees and acutely feel the smaller talent pool and skills shortages.

LEADERSHIP EFFECTIVENESS

There's the adage that employees don't leave organizations; they leave their managers. I host a monthly breakfast in my community for leaders in Human Resources and Learning and Development. Each month, I suggest a topic to focus our discussion. In addition to my topic, leaders bring issues they face, and we lean into our collective wisdom and experience to offer insights and ideas. Recently, a manager shared that he's questioning his commitment to his role. He has stayed because he believes in the company's direction but is frustrated by the misalignment between what he feels is necessary and what his leader prioritizes. They have different values and priorities, and the friction is becoming more than what he wants to bear.

This manager's experience is reflected by a DDI[17] study in which 54% of companies saw their turnover rate increase. The study revealed that employees are 3.5 times more likely to leave when they view their leaders as ineffective. On the flip side, effective leaders have a tremendous positive impact on their teams and organizations. A mortgage lending organization wanted to know if leadership effectiveness impacted business results. They commissioned a study[18] of hundreds of their branches across North America and isolated the factors that influenced business results so they could zero in on leadership effectiveness specifically. They analyzed financial data for each branch and assessed leadership effectiveness through a 360-degree assessment. The study revealed:

- Branches with the bottom-performing branch managers (10%) had a net loss of $1.2 million.

- Branches with average leaders (80%) had a profit of $2.4 million.
- Branches with the most effective managers (10%) had a profit of $4.5 million.

Clearly, leaders affect employee experiences and the organization's success!

While the leader's role is instrumental in retaining and developing employees, it's hard for leaders to be effective and the best versions of themselves when they're burned out, just like their team members. They have pressure from the top and demands from their team. Yet, they need to continue to step into their leadership role because they are the lynchpin between the organization's executive leaders and its employees. They translate strategic goals into team and individual objectives. Leaders need to find a way to rise above these pressures to play the long game – prioritizing learning on their teams alongside meeting company objectives so employees develop new skills and have opportunities to grow. Leaders need a bias for growth that isn't focused on the business but on the person; that isn't about results but about progress.

The benefits of developing employees

The time is now to invest in employee learning and growth. A recent McKinsey report[19] identified that 90% of respondents feel their organizations need to act now or soon to close skill gaps. Yet only 5% responded that their organizations are 'all set' with addressing the capability gaps.

When organizations and leaders value growth through learning and prioritize professional development alongside getting results, they achieve long-term growth instead of short-term results. Companies that invest in their bench strength and develop their future leaders are:

- Six times more likely to be capable of engaging and retaining top talent.
- Five times more likely to be able to prevent employee burnout.
- Three times more likely to be among financially top-performing organizations.[20]

Investing in leaders so they can be effective and create a culture of learning on their team is a significant step in addressing the effects of the global talent shortage. Employees develop new skills they need for today and prepare them for growth tomorrow.

2. The need for better employee engagement

"Train people well enough so they can leave, treat them well enough so they don't want to."

- Richard Branson, Founder of Virgin Group

Recruiting skilled team members, given our talent shortages, is one thing. Keeping employees engaged is another.

Larry[ii] heads up the training department for a medium-sized technology company. In addition to creating and implementing measurable training programs for his organization, Larry is very focused on supporting individual learning and growth. Larry told me of one team member, Barbara, who learned instructional design, including the skills and processes for assessing learning needs. She creatively applied these skills outside of Learning and Development to assess performance issues more broadly. Barbara applied her instructional design skills to an operational context, identified root causes, and recommended solutions for an entirely different department. This analysis garnered Barbara a promotion to a leadership role where she could continue to apply these skills more strategically. Admittedly, Larry was conflicted – his team

---

(ii)   Name has been changed to maintain anonymity.

was all of a sudden short-staffed, yet he was delighted that
his protégée could advance her career.

Leaders benefit from developing their employees because they rise to a higher level of proficiency – they can do more and better work. Yes, the employee may eventually be promoted and leave the team. However, they are less likely to leave the organization because they are learning and engaged.

The prevalence and cost of low employee engagement

Low employee engagement has a tremendous negative effect on organizations' productivity, profitability, and people. When looking across different global geographies, 33% to 60% of employees plan on leaving their jobs.[21] Many of these are 'quiet quitters' detached from their work and organization and are fulfilling their basic job requirements but nothing more.

Gallup estimates that this type of low engagement costs the global economy $8.8 trillion, accounting for 9% of global GDP.[22] What's more, many organizations are unaware of or are out of touch with reality. Most employers falsely believe that less than 20% of their workforce plans to leave.[23] This huge gap between how employees are feeling and what employers are aware of is a blind spot and an area of risk for organizations, especially in our tight labour market.

I see low employee engagement surface when organizations and leaders have a hyper-focus on output. This drive for results excludes other priorities, such as employee learning and development. We can use job satisfaction and job motivation to understand employee engagement and the impact on learning and development.

Frederick Herzberg defined the hygiene theory in the 1960s, which has been expanded upon and is now known as the dual-factor motivation-hygiene theory.[24] This expanded theory looks at job satisfaction and job motivation and identifies different levers for each.

Job satisfaction is met through basic needs such as pay, benefits, and policies that allow for flexible or hybrid work. There's a limit to job satisfaction. More money can move someone from feeling unsatisfied to satisfied, but it can't motivate them to go above and beyond. This is why pay-based incentives have limited success in motivating employees.

When organizations focus on money as a motivator, there's never enough, and employees always want more.

For an employee to be more productive – to move beyond the bare minimum as captured in the term, 'quiet quitter' – they need to be motivated. When organizations focus on employee learning and development, they prioritize growth through learning and tap into employee motivation.

Employees can never get enough growth and, comparatively, it costs very little.

This is especially relevant for small and medium-sized organizations that often struggle to attract and retain employees.[25] They're competing against larger organizations with deeper pockets and more layers that allow for employee promotions.

Instead of offering higher pay and compensation, small and medium enterprises that offer growth through learning can play above their weight and compete with their larger counterparts. Organizations need to establish the basics to achieve baseline employee satisfaction. Then, it's up to the leaders to build on these basics and create a team environment to engage and motivate their people and retain top talent. Seventy percent of team engagement is attributable to the manager.[26] When managers support their employees' continuous learning, employees show greater commitment toward the organization, which reduces their intention to leave.[27]

When we remove learning and growth from our teams, we provide employees with only the basics – pay, benefits, and policies. Work becomes a paycheque. I believe employees want more than an income; they want to grow as individuals, employees, and team members.

The benefits of more engaged employees

When organizations prioritize learning alongside getting results and equip their leaders to create a culture of learning on their teams, employee engagement improves, team performance increases, and organizations thrive. A study by McKinsey[28] shows that organizations focused on both performance and people are more resilient, have higher returns on invested capital, and consistently outperform their peers. These dual-focused organizations also have better retention rates than organizations focused on just performance or neither performance nor people. It's clear that one of the several ways to improve employee engagement and address 'quiet quitters' is to focus on their learning and growth.

I've been working with the leadership team at a medium-sized non-profit organization to help their leaders create cultures of learning on their teams and across their organizations. When I first talked with the VP of Human Resources, she shared that their leaders avoided having career coaching conversations because they were unsure how to broach the subject. They were afraid they would say the wrong thing or unknowingly commit to a course of action contrary to the organization's policies. They felt career conversations were about career advancement, and they didn't want to promise a path to promotion where one didn't exist because of their flat organizational structure. So, they avoided the conversations altogether. Meanwhile, their employees felt there was a limited future for them. So many left. The leaders' hesitancy to have career coaching conversations led to higher turnover, retention challenges, and the need for ongoing recruitment efforts – all of which take time, money, and resources.

3. Rapid technology change

"When we are no longer able to change a situation, we are challenged to change ourselves."

- Viktor E. Frankl

We touched on technology earlier as it relates to skills shortages. Technology and the resulting rapid pace of change is another challenge organizations and leaders are grappling with. Change is upon us and will remain with us. The opportunity that sits before us isn't how to stop change but how we respond as individuals, leaders, and as organizations.

Earlier this year, I facilitated a leadership workshop for a long-standing client. They're a food cooperative, and the participants were starting an 18-month program to develop skills to represent their farms in the organization. In the workshop, leaders worked in teams to complete case studies, apply leadership concepts, and practise skills such as chairing meetings and making presentations. The workshop was multifaceted, so each team had a coach to support them. After the first day, I facilitated a discussion with the coaches to check in on how the groups were doing. We had an interesting conversation about technology. One coach shared that his group was unsure if they could use Google to search for data and resources for their case study. Another shared that their team was using ChatGPT to help them write their report. Upon hearing this, the third coach reacted quite negatively. He wanted to tell his group so they knew another team had an unfair advantage. He felt like the team using ChatGPT was cheating. It was important to him that all of the teams worked within the same parameters, and he wanted to tell his team in order to 'level the playing field.'

I found this conversation and the three coaches' perspectives fascinating. If we take a historical perspective, technology has always provided new tools and ways of doing things – from the printing press to laundry machines to computers. As we explore new technology, we are sometimes asked to adapt more quickly than we're comfortable with. Ten years ago, the group's question about using Google might have elicited a negative reaction and been perceived as cheating. Now, Google is commonplace and considered a go-to research tool. In the 1970s, if a math student used a calculator, they would have been accused of cheating. Now a calculator is a natural extension of math. Suppose we fast forward ten years or even five years. I suspect ChatGPT or another Large Language Model (LLM) will become like the calculator and Google – a tool people have incorporated into their daily lives. The discussion with the coaches and the different perspectives reflect that we're at a transition point with this specific technology. Adapting to new technology represents a change and, as with any change, there are early adopters, resistors, and the majority of us who are somewhere in the middle.

Change as a constant

It seems so obvious a statement: we live, work and learn in a world with constant change. Yes, there has always been change – spring flowers emerge from the thawing soil, the heat of the summer and the slow decay of fall leading into winter. Our lives change, too, as we move from childhood to teenagers and into adulthood. The difference is that the pace and predictability of the change we experience now differs from the seasonal and life stages that are expected. Change is often thrust upon us and is continuous, leaving us with a sense that it will never end. It feels like we can't stop long enough to catch our breath.

When I think of how change can feel, the image of a tornado comes to mind. Tornados are powerful forces of nature that suck up objects in their path and churn and swirl them inside their funnel. If we are faced with change, we are sucked into the tornado, which makes us feel out of control. A small tornado, under the right conditions, can get bigger. As the funnel gets larger, we churn faster. Similarly, a change can feel small initially and grow and start to feel more out of control. Tornados and change aren't going away. Our climate change is making tornados more frequent and more extreme. Our work environment and technological advances are increasing the pace and scale of change in our organizations. Instead of wishing them away, we can look at the conditions that make us feel out of control. Tornados need instability to form – warm, moist air near the ground, and cooler, dry air above. They also need wind to propel them. Applying these concepts to change, we could say that our discomfort with change results from our instability – the difference between how we've worked in the past and what we're being asked to do differently. The greater the difference, the more powerful the tornado and the more discomfort we feel. Like tornados, when there's a strong wind and change happens fast, we can feel more out of control.

I work with a Human Resource leader at a medium-sized municipality. Recently, Colin[iii] shared how his Human Resource team has been struggling to support leaders in managing all the changes being implemented in their organization. Colin talked about a new strategy for the organization, a change in their leadership, and several technology initiatives underway. That's a lot of change all at once! Perhaps you can relate. Change is coming at us from many fronts, and we often don't have the time, skills, or mental bandwidth to respond in a constructive, positive, and supportive way.

(iii) Name has been changed to maintain anonymity.

Like Colin's team, your organization may be experiencing change on many fronts. Technological change is the most rapid and therefore the most challenging to respond to. The World Economic Forum[29] predicts that by 2027, almost half (44%) of workers' core skills will be disrupted.

I worked with Simon,[(iv)] the director of Human Resources at a national law firm, to develop a learning strategy to equip their leaders with skills and resources to coach and develop their employees. When I interviewed their senior leaders, I asked about the pace of change and technology. Many said change and technology were inseparable and they didn't differentiate between the two. Technology equalled change and vice versa.

Think of your organization right now. How many digital transformation initiatives or system changes are underway? The more you have, the larger your tornado and the more your employees will feel out of control. All this uncertainty has a negative impact on productivity, employee commitment, and leadership effectiveness.[30]

Limiting the number of change initiatives may not be within your scope of control, but recognizing the impact and compounding effect of multiple changes on you and your employees is. As leaders, we need to mitigate the instability that feeds the tornado. We need to embed learning into our team cultures so people are curious about, open to, and accepting of changes instead of resistant to them.

_____

(iv)   Name has been changed to maintain anonymity.

Why is change so rapid?

A colleague of mine, Brad Twynham, is a thought leader who focuses on leadership, technology and First Nations' knowledge systems to bring to life the intersection of humanity and technology. I attended one of his sessions[31] where he explained the impact of exponential technology change. Historically, we have experienced linear change, and we've been able to anticipate, respond, and adapt to it. In the past couple of decades, that has changed. Brad shared the following example, which illustrates exponential change and why it's so challenging.

> *Imagine you are in a stadium at a music concert. You are in the 'nosebleed' section – the cheap seats at the top of the stadium, where the stage is a small blip in front of you. Imagine it starts to rain, but instead of a regular rain pattern, each second, the drops double. In the first second, one drop falls; in the second, two raindrops; in the third second, four raindrops, etc. On average, it would take only 25 minutes for the entire stadium to fill. Standing in the nosebleed section, you would see the mosh pit fill in 19 minutes. You'd probably start to wonder if you should leave. The problem is that time is ticking. As you leave your seat with thousands of other people, you have only 3 minutes to evacuate before the entire stadium is filled with water.*

This example highlights that exponential growth is fast, difficult to anticipate, and deceptive. Brad talked about the curve of deception—the point at which the initial slow curve starts to shift up and become rapid change. This curve of deception is when we're in the nosebleed seats, watching the stadium fill and not realizing how quickly it will affect us.

"Exponential change is back loaded and deceptive. Meaning we don't see it coming before it's too late."

- Brad Twynham

Large Language Models (LLMs) are an example of this. ChatGPT exploded into our awareness in late 2022. This represents the curve of deception and when most of us sat up and took notice. In actual fact, research into LLMs has a long history dating back to the 1940s, when researchers were mapping language. The research and science leading up to 2022 were slow and involved incremental change equivalent to the first several drops of rain in the stadium.

As leaders, we cannot possibly anticipate the change we and our teams will need to adapt to. Even if we could see it coming, chances are it will advance faster than we anticipate and can react to. Instead of panicking with the thousands of others trying to get out of the stadium, prepare yourself and your team with a life jacket so when the water reaches you, you can stay afloat while you learn to swim.

4. Resiliency and adaptability

Resiliency and adaptability are your life jackets for dealing with change. Over 60% of leaders across various industries identify that organizational resiliency will be important in the future.[32] And yet half reported their organizations are not well prepared. The rapid pace of change, the need to achieve results, and, with publicly traded companies, pressure to meet shareholder expectations creates a hyper-focus on short-term results. In an environment that prioritizes output – getting results – leaders and their teams need to make decisions fast and act quickly. Leaders default to established processes for efficiency and heuristics, or educated guesses, to simplify and speed up making decisions.[33]

In this environment, there is little time or attention given to learning. Learning means asking questions, pausing to consider new perspectives, and experimenting with different approaches. When there is no room for learning, there is no room for curiosity which creates the environment for innovation.[34] There is no room for making mistakes, which are our greatest opportunities to learn.[35] The bias for speed and action means leaders are less focused on long-term growth. And yet, planning for long-term growth is future-focused. In a future that is increasingly volatile, uncertain, complex, and ambiguous, we need a bias for growth through learning. This prioritizes learning alongside output and results.

There is perhaps no better example of the need to be resilient and adaptable than the COVID-19 pandemic. Organizations had to move their entire workforce to a new way of working. For many, it meant a complete shift to remote work. I don't work in IT, so I can only imagine the extreme efforts needed to recreate the infrastructure, networking, and security to make this possible. Companies moved 40 times more quickly than thought possible, taking, on average, only 11 days to implement a workable remote situation.[37] For organizations that provide essential services, their shift involved finding ways to provide services remotely if possible or in person with safety measures in place. In Canada, doctors offered virtual appointments. My friend, Angela, was diagnosed with breast cancer just as the pandemic started and completed all of her chemotherapy treatments by herself with COVID protocols in place. Thank goodness health care and other essential services found ways of working! Angela's treatment wasn't canceled or delayed. She is now three years cancer-free.

> ### THE DIFFERENCE BETWEEN ORGANIZATIONAL RESILIENCY AND ADAPTABILITY
>
> While both are important, resiliency and adaptability are different. "Resilience refers to the capacity to quickly recover or 'bounce back' from difficulties, while adaptability is the ability to adjust to those difficulties and create something positive from them."[36] Resiliency is like having short-term bursts of energy to run a sprint. Adaptability is like developing increased stamina for a marathon race.
>
> **We need both.**

At the beginning of the pandemic, we all needed resiliency – the ability to adjust to our new ways of working and receiving service. My husband, Dave, works for a global company based in France and has many European colleagues. North America is blessed with space and, in comparison, large homes. Working from home was more manageable for Dave than it was for his European counterparts. He told me that his colleague in Poland juggled work while caring for his toddler and infant. His wife worked in healthcare, so continued to work out of the home. He had to juggle full-time work with parenting in a very cramped apartment. He used an ironing board as his desk in his living room.

We all have personal stories and can recall the extraordinary ones from the pandemic. We all had to be resilient to manage through it. Now, many of the changes that were put in place to cope have become permanently integrated. My doctor still offers virtual appointments. The organizations that held onto the best of the changes have adapted and are now better positioned for future changes and shocks to our system.

There is a strong connection between resiliency and learning.[38] But it's not learning through training programs that leads to growth and adaptability. It's continuous learning in a team culture that encourages curiosity and asking questions, experimenting and learning from failure, and self-discovery with a leader who coaches and guides employees.

The book *The 15 Commitments of Conscious Leadership: A New Paradigm for Sustainable Success*[39] identifies Learning through Curiosity as the second leadership commitment. This commitment emphasizes self-awareness and learning agility. I call this a Learning Mindset, which includes curiosity, courage to take risks to try new things, and consistency – developing a lifelong habit of learning. This is the cornerstone of developing personal and team resiliency and adaptability.

The stadium is filling quickly. Learning provides our resiliency and adaptability life jackets.

The benefits of more resilient and adaptable teams

Organizations that embrace learning are more resilient.[40] When organizations have a growth imperative and move away from a singular focus on output, action, and results, they prioritize learning and growth alongside results. The research that supports this dual focus on people and performance is compelling. These organizations:[41]

- Have more consistent earnings and greater resilience during crises. They are better at retaining talent, with attrition rates 5% lower than those of peer organizations that don't prioritize performance and people.
- Deliver top-tier profitability and are more likely to become large-scale superstars with an average of $1 billion more in economic profit.
- Have a competitive advantage because they challenge and empower employees, which fosters bottom-up innovation. They are 4.2 times more likely than average companies to remain in the top quintile of their sector's return on investment capital (ROIC).[v]

Employees also benefit. The skills employees learn on the job contribute to 46% of their lifetime earnings. The more skills someone acquires, the higher their income.[42] When organizations focus on developing their people, their people benefit and the organization benefits.

As we think of our organizations and the challenges we face, I see both opportunity and risk. The opportunity is that

---

(v) For nine out of 10 years (2010 to 2019).

we *can* embrace employee learning and development. Leaders step into their role in developing cultures of learning alongside achieving results. In doing so, employees and teams become more innovative, resilient, and adaptable. They thrive in the face of constant change because employees are engaged and developing skills for current and future roles. The risk is that organizations look to training departments and learning professionals as the sole source of developing employees and miss the huge opportunity to embed learning into the DNA of their teams. Formal training will only get us part way there. We need both sides of the bridge: formal training under the direction of Human Resources or Learning and Development and a Growth through Learning orientation under the guidance of our leaders.

CHAPTER 2
Training Isn't Working

The ability to adapt is one of those critical evolutionary traits that is core to any successful species, including humans. Adaptability is the key that unlocks our individual and organizational success.

I was watching the Netflix series Life on Our Planet (2023).[43] Season One, episode seven introduces modern-day primates and highlights a significant change in evolution. Mammals and primates in particular have large brains. The episode showed how capuchin monkeys in Costa Rica discovered that rubbing lemons all over their body repelled mosquitos. I imagine monkeys hate biting mosquitos as much as I do, so what a brilliant discovery! Through their advanced brains, they could identify a problem, experiment with solutions, and learn through trial and error what works. Incredibly, they could then teach the new knowledge and skills to other monkeys in the troop. And so, as a troop and as a species, these monkeys learned and adapted.

We adapt and evolve as humans – just like the capuchin monkeys. In our lives and at work, we face challenges, find solutions (often through trial and error), and share our insights with others. Since organizations are made up of individuals, it is through individual learning and growth that organizations grow and adapt.

The need for organizational adaptability is great. There has been no better universal test of adaptability than the COVID-19 pandemic. McKinsey[44] identified that organizations that exhibited healthy, resilient behaviours were better able to withstand the effects of the COVID-19 pandemic. Of organizations with resilient behaviours, 30% were likely to declare bankruptcy in the two years of pandemic disruption, compared to the 73% without resilient behaviours. We may never again have a global crisis of that scale, but the need to be resilient and adaptable – at an individual and organizational level – remains.

The pathway to this adaptability is learning and development. I've worked in learning and development for 25 years, both as an external consultant and heading up the sales training department for North America at a Canadian life insurance company. I believe our workplaces need to provide more than a paycheque. They need to be places where we learn, grow and feel like our contributions matter. I'm passionate about employee, team and organizational growth. I approach this through learning. When facilitating leadership programs, I love it when I see 'light bulbs' go off as leaders gain insights into how their behaviour impacts others. I love working with a struggling team and their leader and helping them build open communication and trust so they can work towards becoming more cohesive and ultimately function better.

Leaders in learning and development are my peeps – my community and network. But, the way employee learning and development is structured and offered in organizations doesn't work. I'm not alone in this. When I talk with clients, I hear frustration about the lack of support they receive for programs. Conferences have a myriad of sessions on how to engage senior leaders and have an impact. A research study by Sehoon Kim et al. highlighted the importance of team learning in organizations.[45] They also identified "limitations to a top-down approach and centralized learning" – the traditional Learning and Development department. Employees need relevant, personalized, and easily digestible content integrated into their regular workday. It needs to be reinforced by coaching and nudges. Learning can't be business-as-usual.[46]

Julianna Morris heads up Porsche People Excellence in Training at Porsche Cars Canada. She's been working in Learning and Development for the past 26 years in various leadership roles.

Over her career, leaders have come to Julianna looking to develop their skills. She shared the example of a leader having problems with critical conversations. They ask her if there's a development course they could take. Julianna pointed out that there are courses, and the descriptions can look great. Leaders can learn concepts and approaches, but without application, mentorship and guidance; without accountability for changing behaviour, it's just a course and has limited impact.

Listen to my conversation with Julianna in my *Growth through Learning* podcast. Go to **www.hannahbrown.co/resources/podcast** or wherever you find your podcasts.

Organizations invest a lot of money, time, and resources on formal training programs. In the United States, corporations and educational institutions spend an average of $954 per employee.[47] Another way to look at this is, on average, large companies have an annual training budget of $16.1 million, medium-size companies have a budget of $1.5 million, and small companies have a budget of $459,177.

Organizations establish training departments to meet compliance and regulatory requirements, onboard new employees, upskill existing ones, and prepare future leaders. Let's take a look at what's not working with this left side of the bridge. In my experience working with hundreds of learning professionals, training departments operate in one of four ways. From least to most effective, they function as a:

1. Cost Centre
2. Service Provider
3. Valuable Contributor
4. Strategic Partner.

1. Training as a cost centre

In its least effective form, the training department functions as a cost centre with employees operating as order takers. The department creates training in response to business demands and internal client requests. The organization may need to comply with legislative changes or regulatory requirements, and it looks to training to meet that need. Courses are topic-focused instead of addressing performance issues. Often, they are hastily designed and don't account for broader factors impacting performance. In a Harvard Business Review article, *Build a Strong Learning Culture on Your Team*,[48] author James McKenna describes these organizations as "still wearing blinders" by focusing on formal classroom training and online modules. He criticizes this approach by highlighting the long lag time between when new skills are needed and when courses are designed and available, the inevitable 'one size fits all' approach, and the lack of support when implementing new programs and learning applications.

When I work with leaders in this type of training department, they describe the frantic pace at which they and their teams must work. They don't have a clear line of sight into the upcoming business needs and so are reacting at the last minute to training requests. They feel frustrated and would like their department to do more, but they feel unable to shift out of reacting and be proactive.

Executives and senior leaders in the organization do not view training as strategic but as a line item on the expense side of the profit and loss statement. There is no measurement of the impact of training beyond 'vanity metrics' such as the number of employees who completed training. Therefore, these leaders often don't know about the possibilities that robust learning can have on employee development and growth.

2. Training as a service provider

Thankfully, not all training departments function as cost centres. Many executives and senior leaders perceive the training function as providing a service. As a service provider, the training manager and their team view themselves as learning and development professionals with expertise in adult education, instructional design, and facilitation. They bring this expertise to bear when supporting their internal clients and the broader organization.

The type of courses typically expand to include supervisor or manager training and a course catalogue for employee personal effectiveness (e.g., communication and mental health). Courses and programs are well-designed and engaging, but they take time to develop. Content creation lags significantly behind the need for that content, making these courses less relevant to the current, specific needs of the audience.[49] They are often still topic-focused instead of addressing a performance need. As such, courses are often generic and don't account for individual learning needs and audience characteristics.

These training managers feel underutilized. They would like their team's courses to be more effective, but receive pushback from their internal business clients, who don't have a full understanding of the instructional design process. For example, the learning and development professionals on these teams want to do a thorough training needs assessment, which would help them design targeted programs, but are asked to pare it down or skip this step altogether.

3. Training as a valuable contributor

A more effective training department provides value to the business beyond meeting compliance or regulatory requirements and providing a catalogue of courses for employees. There is a focus on improving employee performance. The team includes performance consultants who have a broader performance mindset. Their deep expertise helps them apply a learning lens to business and performance needs. They function as consultants who learn about their internal clients and their learner audience, which allows them to identify training and non-training solutions that address performance needs.

While leaders in these training departments provide tremendous value to their internal business clients, they fail to 'have a seat at the table.' They do not provide input into the business strategy and therefore are unable to demonstrate how training can support broad organizational goals and objectives. One of the reasons these leaders struggle is that the lens through which they view internal business clients remains a learning lens. They continue to use the language of learning. They use terms such as 'Kirkpatrick Level 3' when talking about training effectiveness.[50] Their internal business clients don't know what this means, nor should they have to. It's learning and development jargon. Instead, these leaders need to speak the language of business and talk about return on investment and other business metrics. Executives and senior leaders value the service the training department provides but view it as outside of the business strategy and operations.

Many of the learning and development leaders I've worked with lead training departments and teams that operate as valuable contributors to their organizations. I believe this left side of the bridge can do even better.

4. Training as a strategic partner

Finally, when the training manager and team function as learning and development business partners, they deeply understand the business. They know how different functions such as marketing, sales, operations, and finance operate and form a system. They know how they can align training programs to business needs. They are bilingual; they speak the languages of both business and learning. Because they understand the language of business, these leaders and teams design solutions specific to the employees' needs. The learning leader and team work with the business to solve performance and business issues. While solutions have a distinct learning and development focus, they may also include process improvements, organization design ideas, or staffing solutions. These targeted solutions have a specific skill-building focus, account for the employee's work environment, and connect new concepts and skills to their existing tools, processes, and systems. Effectiveness and impact are measured through business metrics in addition to learning metrics. It is, therefore, easier to demonstrate the value of and – dare I say – the return on investment.

As a result, executives and senior leaders view the training function strategically, seeking input in decision-making and when implementing strategic directives.

When I think of the different ways a training department can operate, I picture two boats on a lake. One boat represents the training function; the other represents the business.

When the training function operates as a cost centre, the manager and team are in their training boat as order takers, receiving requests for training. They don't understand the business boat, can't anticipate training requests, and don't add value from a business perspective.

When the training function operates as a service provider with a team of learning and development professionals, they look at what's happening in the business boat to anticipate upcoming requests and align the learning design with the learner audience. They remain in their boat, anchored in their field of expertise.

If the training function operates as a valuable contributor, the team includes performance consultants. The manager and team step out of their boat into the business boat to understand the business and their needs. Then they step back into their boat to design and deliver the training. They easily jump back and forth between the learning and business boats.

Finally, if the training function operates as a strategic partner with learning and development business partners, the leader and team members have one foot in each boat. It's a balancing act, and the boats may drift apart, so they need to work hard to keep them closely aligned. The result, however, is that they can simultaneously understand the business and bring a learning and developing lens to collaborate and jointly solve performance and business challenges.

In his book, *L&D's Playbook for the Digital Age,*[51] Brandon Carson makes a strong case for how learning and development needs to evolve to meet our current political climate. He suggests we need a new approach to the learning and development function – one that places it at the centre of building human capability across the organization. Carson's call to elevate learning and development mirrors my push for training to be a strategic partner. However, he is still focused on the learning and development side of the bridge. Yes, we need our learning function to be more strategic and the formal training programs to be effective, and we need to do a better job of measuring their impact. But, if we continue to focus only on formal training, we will continue to wonder why our programs 'don't stick,' why there is 'poor uptake,' and why behaviour and performance don't change. We need to focus on the other side of the bridge: leader-led employee development. We need team cultures of learning across our organizations so employee learning doesn't remain in the domain of a department but moves into the hands of leaders.

CHAPTER 3
Why Growth through Learning

"Nothing we do is more important than hiring and developing people. At the end of the day, you bet on people, not on strategies."

- Lawrence Bossidy, Former COO of General Electric

To meet the challenges facing our organizations, we need to balance achieving results with developing our people. People are our greatest asset and are the competitive advantage we need to succeed today and be prepared for the future.

Individual learning precedes productivity. It's not an either-or situation. We <u>can</u> balance development and growth, and when we do, we excel.

Developing employees through leader-led learning can occur alongside getting financial results. McKinsey[52] produced a report based on their analysis of just under 2,000 companies in 15 countries around the globe representing a cross-section of sectors. The study examined how much these companies focused on people or performance. It revealed that only 9% of organizations focus on both people and performance, compared to organizations that focus on one or neither. McKinsey labelled these companies as People + Performance (P+P) Winners. Their analysis revealed that the P+P Winners:

- Simultaneously developed employee talent and delivered top-tier financial returns.
- Had greater resilience and more consistent earnings relative to their peers.
- Achieved higher returns on human and organizational capital investment.
- Excelled across these business outcomes: profitability, resiliency, and retention.

While leaders throughout organizations – from executives striving to deliver shareholder quarterly returns to middle managers working to achieve objectives cascaded from their department's strategic goals – may be tempted to focus on getting results at the expense of prioritizing their people, doing so would result in short-term success instead of long-term sustained growth. They would not be in the 9% of the P+P Winners McKinsey identified, and would fall behind their peers.

Growth through Learning Model

The following model illustrates different areas of focus organizations and leaders can have as they work to achieve results. Let me introduce the model here and then go into more detail in subsequent chapters.

Growth through Learning Model

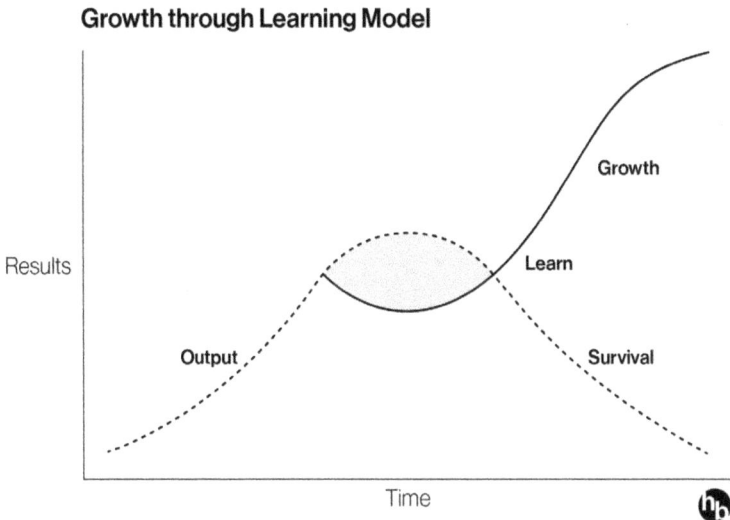

A focus on output leads to surviving

The McKinsey report also identified 21% of organizations as Performance-Driven with a top-down management approach and a goal-oriented culture. I've identified this approach in my model as 'output' to reflect the singular priority on getting results. Whether a manufacturer producing automotive parts, a financial service organization creating and selling products, or a government or nonprofit agency focused on serving its members – an output focus will generate results in the short-term. Output prioritizes getting results over learning and growth. Employees don't learn as many new skills, so the organization becomes ill-prepared for future challenges and opportunities. Over time, the organization slips into survival mode.

A focus on learning leads to growth

To avoid decline and entering survival mode, organizations need to embed learning into the DNA of their teams. Learning in the fabric of an organization's culture, not training from a department, will enable long-term sustainable growth.

This Growth through Learning orientation is an investment that takes time, effort, and ongoing commitment. It's an investment that increases the capability of employees and teams. It requires the commitment to be in the 9% of organizations that McKinsey identified as P+P Winners. When that commitment is made, employees develop new skills and capabilities allowing them and their teams to be higher-performing, innovative and more resilient. [53] The McKinsey P+P Winners also generate greater payoffs for employees. Employees are more likely to move into higher lifetime earnings brackets when working for an organization that devotes time to training and career development.

This approach of employee growth through learning hinges on leaders creating team cultures of learning – infusing development, experimentation, and creativity into their teams. Leaders need to embrace their role of coaching and developing others. This can be difficult, especially if the organization has an output approach to achieving results. Leaders may feel they lack the skills to coach and develop their employees. They may receive mixed messages about the role of a leader as the organization shifts from a culture of output to one of growth. Leaders may also get resistance from their employees. In an output-focused organization, employees are accustomed to working on what's in front of them – the task, project, or initiative. There are tight timelines, little room for error, and high expectations and stress. There is little time to question decisions, challenge assumptions, or find creative, improved ways of approaching situations. In this environment, employees are told what to work on and often how to do it.

The transition to a growth focus, where leaders embrace coaching and developing their employees, turns this on its head. Employees are now asked questions when they surface challenges and issues. They need to think and solve problems, which can be uncomfortable. Employees need to use skills that may have been dormant and underutilized.

Christine Helgerman is the director of St. John's Christian Nursery School and manages a staff of about 15 early learning educators. During the COVID-19 pandemic, there were so many changes in protocols and measures to keep the children safe that the staff developed a habit of checking all decisions with Christine. Christine noticed as the pandemic ended and the protocols lifted, her staff continued to look to her for all decisions. She had to retrain them to think for themselves and make decisions on their own. Instead of providing answers, she asked questions such as, "What do you think?" "What would work best?"

and "What have you already tried?" Over time, Christine's
staff relearned the ability to solve problems on their own
and confidently make decisions within their scope
of control.

Listen to my conversation with Christine in my *Growth through Learning* podcast. Go to **www.hannahbrown.co/resources/podcast** or wherever you find your podcasts.

It may feel easier and more familiar for employees to do what they're told. Following someone else's orders requires less thinking and less risk. It can also absolve the employee of a sense of responsibility for their work and the outcome. Yet, research on accountability in the US Federal government found that increasing accountability directly and positively affected performance.[54] Other research has also found a positive correlation between accountability and improved performance.[55]

So, we want our employees to have a sense of ownership for their work. Leaders need to give up control for that to happen and create space for learning and growth to unfold.

The transition from output to growth is challenging, and yet it is necessary for sustained growth. Of learning and development professionals, 97% percent want to create a team culture of learning in their organizations, yet only 37% have achieved it.[56] Learning is the pathway from output to growth. We can choose to embrace new ideas and learn from mistakes, or we can resist and become further entrenched in an output culture.

A Focus on Output

---

*"A bad system will beat
a good person every time."*

- W. Edwards Deming

CHAPTER 4

An Output-Focused Workplace

No matter the size of your organization or the nature of your business, you are focused on growth – delivering your commitments while being fiscally responsible. Executives of publicly traded companies are held accountable for quarterly earnings and shareholder returns. Privately held, small to medium-sized companies actively pursue growth, often work with slim margins, and are especially sensitive to cash flow. Not-for-profit organizations are subject to donations and grants and need to manage their operational expenses against their sources of funding. Even my clients in government have service-level agreements and public accountability. They, too, need to manage short-term priorities against long-term planning. Municipalities need to balance 30-year strategic plans with shorter-term priorities identified by new councillors in each four-year election cycle. In all these types of organizations, there can be a short-term focus – quarterly results, the next grant cycle, or services funding. The challenge with focusing solely on short-term results is that it doesn't allow for long-term sustained growth. Yes, leaders and employees can rally for a period of time for a specific high-priority goal, but it's not sustainable.

An output focus that prioritizes getting results at the expense of other priorities leads to short-term gains and compromises long-term growth. Let me use a well-known example – the early history of Ford Motor Company – to bring this into focus.

In 1908, Henry Ford created the Model T automobile and proclaimed that he wanted to "build a motor car for the great multitude." He achieved his vision, and by 1921, he was producing 56% of all passenger cars in the United States. He kept the price low, so the Model T was affordable and maintained profits through volume and operational efficiency. Ford became hyper-focused on streamlining production and reduced the time to build one Model T motor car from nine hours and fifty-four minutes to five hours and fifty-six minutes. This singular focus on production time resulted in tuning out other priorities. He missed the consumer need for greater variety. Ford didn't deviate from efficiency and failed to innovate and offer features like conventional gearshifts, hydraulic brakes instead of mechanical ones, and larger cylinder engines. By the late 1920s, General Motors and Chrysler started producing automobiles with these features. They steadily gained market share and, eventually, the Ford Motor Company became third in sales in the industry, falling from number one. Because of his single-minded focus on efficiency, Ford stopped experimenting and innovating and fell behind. Henry Ford prioritized output above all else.

A relentless focus on results leaves little room for other priorities. We know that for organizations to succeed in our socioeconomic and geopolitical environments, they must be resilient and adaptable. They need to overcome labour shortages and low employee engagement. They need to respond to continuous change and technological disruptions. Organizational resiliency and adaptability start with employee resiliency and adaptability. An output focus doesn't allow time to develop new skills. It doesn't have the risk tolerance to experiment and try new things. It doesn't have a long enough time horizon to consider employee career growth. Instead of adapting, employees are stuck in their roles. They don't try new things for fear of making a mistake, and they suffer from it because they lack opportunities to advance their careers.

Sales is one of the functions where we can most directly correlate output and results. Yet, even with salespeople, having an expanded view of results that includes learning and development alongside closing deals leads to better performance. In a study at Southern Methodist University,[57] researchers studied sales professionals to investigate the influence of setting goals on sales performance. The sales professionals worked for a medical supplies distributor and had, on average, 10 years of experience. So, they weren't newbies. In the study, the sales professionals promoted a new product and could earn a significant bonus for each unit they sold. They were motivated to get results. The researchers found that the sales professionals who created learning goals (e.g., cooperation with colleagues, experimentation, and developmental feedback) instead of performance goals (e.g., competition between colleagues, punishment for mistakes, evaluative feedback) were far more successful.

I find this fascinating. Most of my husband's career has been in sales. I've watched his career unfold and witnessed his successes and failures. I would have thought that focusing on the outcome – performance – would lead to more wins than losses. And yet, a broader focus on learning leads to better performance. As leaders, we can apply this to how we lead and motivate our teams, whether we are in sales or a different functional area. In fact, the researchers concluded and recommended, "When managers have a choice between using management practices that are likely to encourage a learning or performance goal orientation, the former is more likely to result in productive outcomes."

On the surface, setting learning goals seems contrary to getting results. Learning takes time and includes risks and often failure. The natural instinct is to set outcome-based goals and 'keep the eye on the prize,' so to speak. However, this study and Ford's approach to producing the Model T suggest that a different, more encompassing approach to getting results is more effective. Leaders and organizations need to focus on growth through learning.

We can also look at another, more recent example of an organization hyper-focused on output: the rise of Tesla Inc. and Elon Musk's relentless focus on output. Mass producing electric vehicles (EVs) served him well initially. Now that hyper-focus on output is moving the organization into survival mode.

In Tesla's early days, the company focused on creating and producing mass market electric vehicles (EVs). Their mission was "To accelerate the advent of sustainable transport by bringing compelling mass-market electric cars to market as soon as possible."[58] This was an audacious goal inspired by Elon Musk that employees, early investors and shareholders rallied behind. To accomplish this, employees worked extremely long hours, often late into the night and through weekends.[59] Corners were cut in the workplace, with numerous reports of unsafe environments, harassment, and reports of high-stress levels among employees.[60] Despite these challenges, this intense focus on output enabled Tesla to survive in its early years. The company broke through barriers and forever changed the global automotive industry.

Once the prototype Tesla Roadster was revealed in 2006, the company turned to mass production in 2008.[61] The relentless focus on results shifted from design and prototyping to producing vehicles at scale. Buoyed by the success of the Tesla Roadster, employees continued to rally. They were a motivated workforce, supportive of the Tesla vision and the passion of their leader, Elon Musk. However, this motivation was difficult to sustain in the face of continued high-pressure demands. Over time, the intense workload and lack of work-life balance led to burnout and decreased morale among employees. Reports of workers fainting from exhaustion and enduring hazardous working conditions further eroded motivation. The fear of making mistakes and the constant pressure to perform created a toxic environment where employees felt undervalued and overworked.[62]

As the company grew, workplace safety became a significant concern. Between 2014 and 2018, the Fremont,

California plant had three times as many Occupational Safety and Health Administration (OSHA) violations as that of 10 other major US auto plants, (such as BMW, Nissan, Toyota, and Ford) combined. Injuries were higher than the national average, and Tesla was repeatedly found to have misclassified and underreported injuries.[63] This focus on output and meeting production targets at the expense of safety created an environment where employees regularly faced significant physical risks.

On the surface, Tesla continued to achieve results – its sales continued to increase. The company's aggressive production goals led to some periods of financial success, including the record-setting number of sales in 2019, which generated $24.6 billion in revenue. However, these gains were often overshadowed by significant losses. Despite the high revenue, Tesla lost $862 million in 2019. The company had back-to-back profitable quarters for the first time in its history, but this was often achieved through the sale of regulatory credits rather than sustainable operational profits.[64] While sales were increasing, Tesla's profitability consistently suffered. The relentless focus on production at the expense of employee development and well-being has led to marginal success – revolutionizing the vehicle market and increasing sales, yet limited to no profitability through to the end of 2019.[65] Since then, Tesla's revenue has continued to climb, but its profitability margin remains just over 25%, and even this is largely due to carbon credit sales.[66] As of 2023, the gross and operating margins were down, indicating the profitability of the company's operations continue to struggle.[67]

Elon Musk's leadership approach has heavily influenced Tesla's culture. His demand for perfection, relentless effort from employees, and the need to get results are often at the expense of employee health and well-being. Musk's direct and demanding leadership style fosters a culture of fear, where employees are afraid to speak out or make mistakes. This leadership approach, while driving short-term gains and pushing the company through critical phases of development, has ultimately led to a high turnover rate and a demoralized workforce. [68]

There are echoes of Ford's Model T rise and fall in Tesla Inc. – aside from both involving automotive companies. Like Henry Ford, Elon Musk shifted focus after the initial design to a hyper-focus on output. Tesla critics point out that the initial design hasn't changed since 2012, making the design over ten years old, which is unheard of in the automotive industry, where most manufacturers replace a model after seven or eight years. [69] *As the only manufacturer of EVs in 2012, Tesla enjoyed a monopoly, so this perhaps wasn't a concern. But now that other automotive manufacturers have entered the EV space and provide a broad range of EV models, competition will create additional pressure on Tesla to innovate while further streamlining its production. Tesla still dominates the EV market in North America, but models from other manufacturers have already impacted its market share, dropping Tesla Inc. from 79.4% in 2020 to 65.4% in 2022.* [70] *"With Tesla's innovation advantage completely erased, there is nothing to stop the big manufacturers from taking over the EV market."* [71]

As with Ford Motor Company in the 1920s, Tesla's culture and extreme focus on production after the initial EV design could continue eroding its market share. The company could move from an output focus to survival mode. "At most, it seems that Tesla can only aspire to survive – and become yet another car manufacturer."[72]

An output focus reflects a broader organizational culture defined and reinforced by leaders and employees alike. Let's look at leadership behaviours and employee experiences in this type of environment.

CHAPTER 5
How Leaders Reinforce an Output Focus

When I think of people working in organizations, I think of head, heart, and hand. The 'top of the house' executives, who set the strategy and make the decisions, are the heads. The frontline employees doing the work are the hands. The leaders who manage teams are the lynchpin that hold the organization together. They translate what the head decides so the hands can implement it. These managers are the heart. To carry this analogy further, you could say as the heart, managers pump the blood through the body; they maintain the flow of information. In a more abstract way, as the heart, they hold the feelings for the body. Organizations are institutions – things. As the heart, leaders are the human side of the 'institutional' organization, bringing it to life. Leaders translate the abstract intellectual concept of the organization into a lived experience for employees.

Being the heart in an output-focused organization is challenging. For new managers, the move from an individual contributor role to a management role involves shifting from relying on expertise and often years of experience doing the work, to managing others doing the work. The skills needed to manage others are different and perhaps new and in need of further development. In an output-focused environment, there is little room to learn and practise these new skills. It's 'sink or swim.' There is no room for error, so trying to test new skills and coach and develop employees feels too risky. Instead, leaders double down on what they know and have been successful with in the past: doing the work and being the hands.

> *Janice[vi] is an innovation manager for an academic institution in the United States. She traces her leadership roots back to her college years and a series of leadership roles of increasing responsibility. She generously shared the experiences and challenges she had as a new leader.*
>
> *In 2016, Janice was early in her career as a leader and was working for a growing tech company in Silicon Valley. As a scaling tech company, the organization's culture was fast paced with high stakes. The pressure from the executive team was significant. Janice was overseeing a new product launch, and the narrative was, "This launch needs to be successful, or the company will fail." The launch was struggling, and so Janice went to India to oversee things directly. She didn't have expertise in the technical aspects of the product, so struggled to find the solutions they needed. She managed through it and the launch was marginally successful.*

(vi)   Name has been changed to maintain anonymity.

As a more mature leader now looking back on that experience, Janice realizes she should have flown in experts who had the required technical knowledge. She had two people on her team, so could have easily done this. They could have worked together to find a solution, which would have resulted in a more successful product launch. At the time, however, Janice was trying to take control of a situation over which she felt she had no control. The more she didn't know, the more she tried to control things. It was a vicious downward cycle. "Trying to take control is a horrible instinct", Janice shared. She's right; it increases stress levels and leads to impulsive decisions and an inability to see the nuances of a situation to identify creative solutions. As a new leader, she didn't need the technical expertise; her role was to lead her team.

When I asked what caused her to cling to control and not invite her team members to collaborate, Janice shared that it stemmed from the need for perfection – to be better and more capable – and, ultimately, from feeling like an imposter.

Janice's story highlights the challenges leaders, especially new leaders, face as they develop in their leadership role. There's a misconception that the leader needs to be the technical expert. When they aren't, like Janice, they can feel out of control. They haven't developed the skills or realized their role is to guide others doing the work. Leaders hold onto control and double down on trying to be the experts. Janice's situation led to her feel like an imposter. "I'm supposed to have the technical skills to manage this launch successfully, but I don't. What kind of a leader am I if I can't do this?"

In my work with leaders and in my research for this book, control, ego, and lack of time emerged as challenges leaders face in an output-focused organization. These challenges shape their behaviour and how they lead their teams.

Controlling behaviour

Successful employees are regularly promoted into management roles because of their technical expertise. Often, they struggle to shift from doing the work themselves to getting it done through others.

> *Dennis[(vii)] had a very successful career in technical sales and client strategy for a global technology company. He was mid-career and had been with the company for 15 years when he was offered a position to lead an international team. It took Dennis six months to realize that he needed to delegate and learn how to tap into the expertise of his team members to get the work done instead of doing it himself. Until he figured that out, he was swamped, trying to manage everyone and everything.*

Individual contributors are the hands – they get the work done. They work best when they control the work they do and the details of how to do it. They don't control the bigger picture, the larger perspective or the broader objective, but they have

---

(vii) Name has been changed to maintain anonymity.

control over their work. This sense of control, or autonomy, contributes to their internal motivation.[73] When moving into a leadership role, managers no longer have control over how the work gets done. Instead, they have control over the objectives and direction of the team. When you're accustomed to controlling the work, giving that up and refocusing on the larger objective can be challenging.

The challenges of letting go of doing the work can be further exacerbated with middle managers who are not strategic decision makers in the organization. Senior leaders make strategic decisions, so some managers may feel that in addition to not controlling the details of the work, they also don't control the overall direction. As the proverbial 'middle manager,' they are squeezed and may feel rudderless or like a cog in a machine. This is fertile ground for leaders trying to regain a sense of control and tightly managing how employees do their work. Instead, they need to replace control over doing the work with control over their leadership and how they coach and develop their employees. It is through leading with learning that employees grow. Employees gain new skills, have a sense of autonomy, and feel pride in their work because they are encouraged to use their expertise.

To be clear, the struggle to balance doing the work versus managing others doing the work isn't limited to new managers. I worked with an executive leadership team at a smaller organization of under 500 employees. They shared their struggle to find this balance. They felt they were hired for their technical skills in addition to their leadership capabilities. The smaller size of their organization created an expectation that they do the work alongside their team members in addition to leading at a strategic level. Even at this senior level, there is an opportunity for these senior leaders to shift how they lead. They need to stop being the hands and, in this case, be the mind of the organization. The more time spent as hands, the less time they have to set the strategic direction for the company.

Ego and hero behaviour

"Hire people who are better than you are, then leave them to get on with it. Look for people who will aim for the remarkable, who will not settle for the routine."

– David Ogilvy, Advertising Executive

The other theme I've observed in my work with leaders and heard in my interviews is the role of the ego in driving leaders' actions. Moving from being the hands to being the heart or even the mind of an organization involves a change of identity, which the ego may resist.

As an individual contributor, an employee is an expert in their work. They've developed mastery and feel a sense of satisfaction for work well done. Their identity and ego are centred on the quality of their work and expertise in their field. The 'expert identity' sounds like:

- I know how to do this.
- I'm the best person to do this work.

- I've done this hundreds of times and know I'll be successful.
- I'm confident in my ability to do this work.
- I haven't solved this exact problem, but it's like other work I've done, so I know I can find a way.

As high performers, these experts are promoted into manager roles where their deep expertise has less value. Their scope of responsibility has increased, so they need a broad perspective instead of deep knowledge. When experts hold onto their expert identity in their leadership role, it becomes a 'hero identity.' They hold onto doing the work when they should let go. Dopamine is one of the hormones responsible for the pleasure part of our brain. There's a dopamine rush in being in the centre of the work. It can be tremendously rewarding to be involved in the details of work – to be in the middle of things. As leaders, we may hold onto this 'doing' because of the dopamine rush it gives us. This can lead to a 'hero identity' where the leader feels compelled to do the work alongside their team members. The 'hero identity' sounds like:

- There's so much going on; my team needs me to step in and help.
- I can't delegate this because my team doesn't know how to do it.
- I can do it faster and better, so I'll just do it.
- I've put out so many fires today. It's stressful, but it feels good that I could help so much.
- I can't imagine my team being able to do this without me.

- My team appreciates it when I step in to help.
- My manager better see how busy we are. I'm indispensable and valuable.

The problem is that working with a hero identity isn't sustainable. These leaders work long hours, have high stress, and don't feel like they can 'unplug.' The risk of occupational burnout increases when employees work over 50 hours per week, and increases even more substantially at 60 hours per week.[74] These are leaders who take their laptops on vacation and check their cell phones while on the beach. The business environment is constantly changing. Therefore, leaders need to be more than just competent in performing tasks or having technical expertise.[75] They need to recognize their strengths and be aware of their limitations. They must surround themselves with team members who have expertise, knowledge and skills that complement their shortcomings and create a well-rounded team.

I introduced Adam Stephens in Chapter One as the director of Marketing and Community Engagement at The Humane Society of Kitchener Waterloo & Stratford Perth. Adam shared that caring for employees as people is at the core of his leadership approach. He is curious, which leads to empathy and an overall caring approach to leading others. I asked Adam if he was always such an empathic leader, and he shared a pivotal point in his leadership journey that shaped how he leads now.

> *Adam had hired a front-end web developer who was taking the lead on the website strategy and redesign. Adam thought he had a pretty good sense of what was needed and what the strategy should be. He was outlining his*

perspective in a meeting with his web developer. After getting the gist of his approach, she interjected and said, "Absolutely not," then proceeded to draw out his process on a whiteboard to illustrate how it would collapse. Adam described a moment where he was watching her and realizing she was completely right. His approach would have been catastrophic. He realized she was smarter than he was. In that moment, Adam learned if you trust someone enough to hire them, you need to trust them when working together. He needed to let go of control, not be the expert, and step aside to allow his team member to shine.

Listen to my conversation with Adam in my *Growth through Learning* podcast. Go to **www.hannahbrown.co/resources/podcast** or wherever you find your podcasts.

It took courage for Adam to realize his limitations, be open to his employee's perspective, and value her contribution. He could have stood firm in his conviction that he was the expert and knew what was best. He could have unnecessarily inserted himself into directing the solution so he could maintain a hero identity and feel a sense of worth and accomplishment for his contribution in defining and implementing the strategy.

"It doesn't make sense to hire smart people and then tell them what to do. We hire smart people so they can tell us what to do."

- Steve Jobs

As long as leaders hold onto their identity as capable 'doers,' they get their dopamine rushes and feel like heroes. This prevents them from forming new identities as leaders who coach and develop others. They need a new source of satisfaction – that of supporting others. When that is fully embraced, leaders can let go of the need to control. As Janice experienced, they can let go of the feelings of inadequacy and embrace coaching and developing employees to achieve growth through learning.

Time and scarcity behaviour

Another theme with leaders is a feeling of scarcity from a lack of time. From executives to middle managers to front-line supervisors, everyone struggles with not having enough time to get their work done and accomplish their objectives.

I challenge this narrative for two reasons. First, in our fast paced, ever-changing workplaces, there will never be enough time. Years ago, my good friend from university returned to work after having her first child. Ruth observed that she would never finish her 'to-do' list and that it would all be waiting for her the next day when she returned to work. If you're like Ruth, you have a long to-do list! Ruth decided to let go of the need to finish everything and accept that her days would end with unfinished tasks. The narrative of "I don't have enough time" isn't helpful. Instead, like my friend Ruth, we need to accept or even embrace this as our reality. This means sitting in some discomfort with the unfinished items waiting for us.

The second reason I challenge the time narrative is because I think it's more about priorities than time. For example, if your day is full and your furnace breaks down in the dead of winter, or your child is sick, you somehow find the time to call and wait for the technician or take your child to the doctor. More time doesn't appear in your day. You automatically rearrange your priorities to make room for the technician or the doctor's visit. When we truly need time, we find it.

When we are caught in a scarcity mindset and feel there isn't enough time, our minds fall into traps that undermine our ability to lead effectively.[76] First, scarcity thinking causes us to fixate on the presenting issue – finish a report, close more deals, etc. Scarcity compels us to focus on the urgent and often neglect the important.[77] We respond to emails instead of completing a grant application. Fixating on scarcity and focusing on the urgent interrupts our higher-order thinking. This is the second trap we fall into. Cognitive load is the amount of mental effort we expend. When we fixate on scarcity, our cognitive load increases; we expend more mental energy and become stressed. Scarcity creates a high cognitive load by constantly pulling our attention away from higher-level thinking to unmet, urgent needs.

Having a scarcity mindset is tiring. All the stress wears us down, and we experience what researchers call 'decision fatigue.' Decisions become increasingly difficult to make throughout the day as mental resources are depleted. In this state, we are more prone to making irrational, trade-off decisions, such as staying up to 2:00 am to finish a report. Your mind isn't as sharp when it's that tired, and so it takes twice as long to do the work. Instead, going to bed and getting up early means it would take a fraction of the time to finish the report.

A scarcity mindset can create a vicious cycle. Scarcity often begets more scarcity based on our limited ability to make sound, reasonable decisions. Yet, it is possible for leaders to step out of this cycle and choose to lead differently.

> *As the corporate controller at a medium-sized food and beverage manufacturer, Olive[viii] leads a team of four managers, each with direct reports for a full team of 14 reporting to her. Her professional development journey started with working for an autocratic leader who wasn't inclined to explain 'the why' of doing things. There was little opportunity to learn other than in the little time she could carve out for herself from her busy day. Olive always prioritized learning and continued her education alongside working, obtaining her CPA in 2023. So, when Olive started leading others, she prioritized one-on-one meetings, check-ins, and conversations about roles and processes. She also described receiving candid feedback about her leadership approach, which further caused her to evaluate how she approached these conversations.*
>
> *The combination of her early autocratic leader, her pursuit of further education, and the feedback she received about her own leadership style has resulted in Olive prioritizing employee coaching and development conversations. She agrees there's little time in her day and that it's a challenge to balance competing demands, but she has identified these conversations as a priority.*
>
> *Olive talked about the benefits of spending time with her team. Her leadership approach encourages two-way discussion, which further builds the relationship and increases*

(viii) Name has been changed to maintain anonymity.

*input from others, leading to new ways of thinking and
more creative solutions. Her team culture is one where it is
safe to talk, share ideas, and speak up. Olive shared that
her team members benefit because they feel safe and they
want to come to work. They feel like they can influence the
team and the organization.*

Olive's story provides an example of how to overcome a scarcity mindset and a continued sense of too little time. Olive also shared that her leadership approach is cascading throughout her team. In prioritizing her people alongside their performance, Olive is role-modelling her leadership approach to her managers. They, in turn, are prioritizing coaching with their teams.

For leaders, this ongoing sense of not having enough time can be exacerbated by a need for control and by holding onto their hero identity. Earlier, I shared Dennis' experience of learning to delegate to his team. He shifted from doing the work to getting work done through others. Unfortunately, some managers never make this transition. It could be their need for control. It could also be the culture they work in and the role models they've had in their careers.

*I work with a senior manager in a medium-sized
municipality. We were discussing the development needs of
their front-line supervisors, and lack of time came up as one
of the challenges these supervisors struggle with. We talked
about the transition from doing to managing and how
the supervisors often hold onto doing the work. He then
shared this quote an employee provided in their employee*

> *engagement survey: "Our supervisor consistently goes to bat*
> *for us. This person makes sure we all receive acknowledge-*
> *ment for our successes and doesn't steal those victories. I*
> *feel safe and supported to make mistakes. I also feel that my*
> *supervisor is not afraid to do the grunt work and this work*
> *is not 'below' them."*

What great insight this quote provides about this work culture! It's beautiful this employee feels so supported by their supervisor. And yet the comment indicates a culture where good leadership is defined by supervisors stepping into operational tasks. This helps their employees with the time crunch of the moment – of many moments – but it reinforces a pattern of managers doing operational tasks, not leadership tasks. These supervisors have less time because they step in to help their staff. The more they step in, the more they reinforce the message that leaders do operational tasks. The more they step in, the less their staff solve problems for themselves, and the fewer new skills they develop. The more they step in, the more short-term results they're supporting.

Leaders and their teams work in organizations with rules, expectations, norms, and patterns of interaction. If the employee who shared this quote moves into a supervisor role, they will undoubtedly be a leader who 'does the grunt work' Since this was role modeled for them and reflects what this organization's culture values. The culture in which leaders operate, the expectations of them and the role models they've had, shape and guide their approach to leadership.

For a leader to shift out of a role of doing and into manag-ing, they need the courage and internal resolve to be a leader who leads through learning – coaching and developing their employees. They need to let go of controlling the details of the work and discard the hero identity. Leaders need to reprioritize their time to make space for developing others so their teams become more capable and higher performing and so they can focus on more strategic work.

When leading with an output focus, leaders become singularly focused on getting results at the expense of other priorities, such as learning, building relationships, and creating downtime to decompress and de-stress. They achieve results in the short term but at the expense of long-term sustained growth. This is supported by the McKinsey[78] study I introduced in Chapter One. McKinsey analyzed companies according to how they focused on performance and/or people. Of the companies, 21% were categorized as performance-driven. While these companies had comparable profitability with the Performance + People (P+P) winners, they lagged in revenue growth and earnings over time. In stable economic times, performance-driven companies can be as successful as the P+P winners. However, they have increased exposure to volatility and risk in turbulent times. We are in turbulent times now! We have a shortage of workers and a growing gap between the skills we need and the skills employees have. We are facing constant change and technology disruption. Organizations need to move past output and adopt a Growth through Learning orientation where leaders coach and develop their people.

CHAPTER 6

Employees in an Output-Focused Workplace

W orking in an environment with a hyper-focus on output is stressful. Robin is the director of Corporate Training Services at Durham College in Toronto. When we talked, he reflected on past roles he's had leading teams in learning and development.

> *Robin explained that one of his previous employers was top- and bottom-line focused – top-line focused on increasing revenue, and bottom-line focused on reducing expenses. Leaders were expected to push their teams and employees to get results, to the detriment of their people. He shared a story of one employee who's struggling. She used to report to Robin and now reports to another manager. When working with Robin, if she made a mistake, she would tell him and ask for help to fix it. They would discuss what happened and find a way to correct it. Now, when she makes a*

mistake, she doesn't say anything. She doesn't tell her new manager. She hides it because she's too afraid to speak up.

Robin and the culture at his former organization provide a great example of how an overemphasis on output can negatively impact an employee's work experience, their performance, and ultimately the organization's ability to achieve the very results they're striving for.

Listen to my conversation with Robin in my *Growth through Learning* podcast. Go to **www.hannahbrown.co/resources/podcast** or wherever you find your podcasts.

Growth Equation

Years ago, I created the Growth Equation[79] to assess what employees need to be successful in their roles. I've used it for many years in learning and development to determine if a training course is the best solution to address a performance need. I've also used it with leaders as a tool to determine how they can support their employees' growth and development. It's also a useful framework to understand an employee's experience in an output-focused work environment.

There are six factors employees need to be successful in their job. These factors form a mathematical equation because if one factor is missing, growth will be zero. Let me explain the framework and then use it to describe an employee's experience working in an output-focused workplace.

Growth is a function of:

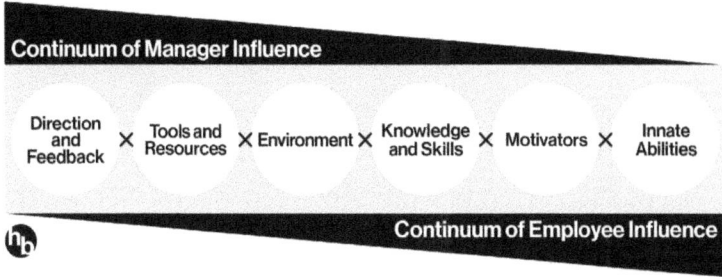

Continuum of Manager Influence					
Direction and Feedback	× Tools and Resources	× Environment ×	Knowledge and Skills	× Motivators ×	Innate Abilities

Continuum of Employee Influence

Direction and Feedback

First and foremost, employees need clear direction and feedback from their manager. They need to know what is expected of them and what their priorities are. As they do their work, they need feedback on what they're doing well and what they should do differently. Research has shown that when employees know their responsibilities, they will be more accountable, which will lead to an increase in their performance.[80]

Tools and Resources

Employees also need tools and resources to be successful. These include tangible things like a computer, desk, and software. They also include access to information, budget, and established processes and procedures.

Environment

Third, employees need a safe environment in which to work. They must be physically safe and confident that they will be able to work without harm or injury. Research[81] has shown that "employees' safety and health are of primary importance, as both are key elements in achieving an organization's desired productivity and efficiency." Employees also need to feel safe psychologically and emotionally, which is why diversity, equity, and inclusion (DEI), anti-harassment, and health and safety policies and programs are so important. Psychological safety helps teams realize the positive impacts of their diversity as well as their potential in higher performance and well-being.[82]

The Growth Equation shows a continuum of influence for leaders and employees. These first three factors are where the manager has a direct impact on the employee's growth. Starting on the left with direction and feedback and moving to the right, the leader has an important role in ensuring these factors are in place for their employees.

Knowledge and Skills

The fourth factor that affects employee growth is knowledge and skills. Employees need the baseline knowledge, experience, and education to do their job. As outlined in Chapter One, leaders are finding it increasingly difficult to hire the people with the skills and expertise they need. More than baseline knowledge, employees need specialized skills in order to be successful in their current job and to position them for success in future roles which will emerge out of our changing digital landscape.

Motivation

The fifth factor is motivation. To be motivated we must feel competent, have a sense of connection and security, and have a sense of autonomy.[83] People are motivated externally and internally. An externally motivated employee works for an external reward, like a bonus. When internally motivated, an employee works because they enjoy it and get personal satisfaction from doing it. I can think of instances where I've worked well beyond what was expected of me because I was enjoying it.

In Chapter One, I introduced the dual-factor hygiene model (a dreadfully academic name, I know!), which explains different factors that affect job satisfaction and motivation. Basic needs (job, pay, benefits, etc.) are externally motivating, and have limited effectiveness in motivating employees. While leaders have a greater impact on these external motivators, they can't rely on them alone. They need to tap into their employees' internal motivators to truly engage them.

As Daniel Pink outlines in his book, *Drive*,[84] there are three conditions that affect internal motivation.

- Autonomy – We want to feel in control and able to take direct action that results in real change.
- Mastery – We want to gain different skills and achieve a level of competency.
- Purpose – We crave a sense of belonging and attachment to others.

In addition to motivating employees, these conditions create a positive team culture.

Innate Ability

Finally, the sixth factor that employees need to perform and grow in their role is innate ability. This factor is more controversial because of the ongoing, unresolved debates in psychology, sociology, and biology about nature versus nurture. Let me explain with an example. In Canada, there are 560,000 minor hockey players registered with the Hockey Canada Foundation.[85] Many are very talented and advance through House Leagues to AAA competitive leagues. The players that progress to increasingly competitive leagues have the factors in the Growth Equation. They are motivated and have the skills and knowledge to play the game. They've likely been raised in a supportive environment and provided with the tools and resources to develop their skills. Their coach and parents would have provided them with direction and feedback throughout their hockey careers. And yet, only one in four thousand will make it to the NHL (National Hockey League). There is an element of innate ability that affects their performance and growth. Innate ability affects performance, but it's just one of the six factors and is the last factor to consider.

These last three factors are where the employee has a direct impact on their performance and growth. The manager can influence these factors indirectly, but the employee has the most control. Let's use the Growth Equation as a lens to understand an employee's experience in an output-focused workplace.

Growth Equation in an Output-focused Workplace

Environment, Knowledge and Skills, and Motivation are the factors most impacted by an output-focused workplace. Tesla Inc. provides one example of an environment in an output workplace. Janice, in Chapter Five, provides another. You may also have your own experiences where you worked in a fast-paced, high-stakes, stressful workplace. Initially performance and results are sufficient, but this environment takes its toll over time. Employees, including leaders, have higher stress levels and more challenges with mental health.[86] Shortcuts lead to a less safe workplace, and the incidents of injury increase.[87] The environment in an output-focused workplace makes sustained growth impossible.

An output-workplace also negatively affects the knowledge and skills factor in the Growth Equation. When all the priorities are on getting results, there is little room to experiment, make mistakes, and learn from failures. Research shows we learn best when we face challenges, make mistakes and need to innovate and adapt.[88] [89]

Finally, an overemphasis on output negatively impacts employee motivation. Initially, motivation may be quite high in an output-focused workplace. Employees rally behind a cause – a singular focus – and get a sense of satisfaction for their contribution to the team's or organization's success. They have a sense of purpose, which, as outlined earlier, is one of three contributors to motivation. The difficulty is in maintaining motivation over a prolonged period of time. As you read with Tesla Inc., over time, employee engagement and morale suffer and turnover increases. More time, money, and effort are spent on employee recruitment, hiring, and orientation. It's estimated that the cost to hire an employee is three to four times their salary.[90] So, while top-line revenue may grow – sales increase, number of customers increases – the cost of production also increases. Overall profitability declines. Again, Tesla Inc. provides a clear example of this.

We know that organizations, whether business, non-profit, or government institutions, need to grow to remain viable in our ever-changing environment. When organizations are hyper-focused on results, they prioritize output above all else. They achieve results over the short term, but achieving long-term sustained growth is next to impossible. Leaders are reacting and struggle to maintain control, which can lead to micromanaging. Their identity is wrapped up in doing operational tasks instead of strategic work, and, as a result, they don't have enough time to do their work.

Through the lens of the Growth Equation, employees struggle to work effectively in an output-focused workplace. There is little room to gain new knowledge or develop new skills. Their motivation to continuously put in long hours and go above and beyond wanes as they feel burned out, stressed, and disconnected from the purpose of their work.

CHAPTER 7
Survive

I f organizations don't move out of an output focus, they plateau and decline. They become focused on surviving.

According to the Standard & Poor's (S&P) 500 Index, the average lifespan of a company eighty years ago was 67 years. Now, it's 15 years.[91] There are several reasons for this, including the challenges I outlined in Chapter One and a singular focus on output.

Organizations need to increase their capability, which requires learning embedded in the DNA of teams. They also need the ability to adapt to changing environments, which requires creativity, innovation, and resilience to achieve long-term sustained growth. When organizations fail to build capacity and grow through learning, they become one of the many that don't exist past 15 years.

Martha[ix] is a senior human resource leader at a global manufacturing organization. The leaders at one of their

---

(ix)   Name has been changed to maintain anonymity.

facilities have a short-term, results-focused approach to leading their teams. As a manufacturer, there's pressure to get parts out the door while meeting the terms of the contract and adhering to safety and quality standards. Martha's description of these leaders reminded me of the Henry Ford story I shared in Chapter Four. The leaders were focused on output at the expense of other priorities.

One of the overlooked priorities in this facility is employee development and succession planning. Leaders view their employees as a predefined collection of skills and capabilities, and they don't see the potential in their employees for future, more advanced roles. When a position needs filling, leaders hire externally. They haven't developed employees internally, so don't have suitable candidates who can easily step into the vacant role. In the few instances where a technical operator could be promoted to a supervisor role, leaders don't want the hassle of backfilling the operator position. They'd rather leave the operator in their current role and hire for only the vacant position. As a result, when a technical operator is ready for a new position, they leave the organization.

These teams have high turnover, chronic staff shortages, and a high proportion of new employees learning the job. Overall, they are not performing at their fullest potential. Employees don't stay because there is no future for them to grow, learn, and develop. The high turnover leads to a loss of institutional knowledge – the intricacies of running a machine or the specific insights into a customer. The manager spends a disproportionate amount of time recruiting employees.

Overall, there is a downward spiral effect. The remaining employees see no future for themselves and have no hope of career advancement. They are not motivated to stay, so there is less incentive to do quality work. Their leaders aren't investing in them, so they in turn don't invest in the company. Over time, there is a negative feedback loop or self-fulfilling prophecy – employees aren't valued, learning, or motivated to do quality work, so they have mediocre performance. Leaders expect less of their employees because of their mediocre performance. When leaders expect less of their employees, employees continue to put in less effort. Quality and production continue to decrease.

What Martha's story highlights is the central role the leader has in shaping the culture of the team and the employee's experience. It also illustrates the negative spiral that can quickly take root.

Leaders in this environment don't see how their leadership creates and perpetuates the problem. I use a diagnostic with leaders to assess their learning mindset and approach to team culture. One question asks how the leader responds when faced with consistent challenges or pain points. Leaders in this situation accept the status quo and believe the challenges are part of the job. Or, they are aware the situation could be different but are unsure of how to change.

Leaders in this state don't take responsibility nor connect their actions to the team's performance. They recognize their team's performance is sub-optimal but look to others to solve the problem instead of looking internally. These leaders are inclined to send an employee to a training course to "get them fixed" thereby putting the onus on Human Resources and the employee for performance improvement. Yet, we know formal training programs only go so far. When the manager actively supports the employee attending a training course, the employee's ability to apply what they learned increases by 94%. Improved performance follows.[92] The manager has a critical role in supporting formal training programs and creating a team culture of learning, which includes coaching and leader-led development. This is not the responsibility of Human Resources, and employees can't do it on their own. To create a team culture of learning requires a learning mindset and a team culture. It requires the organization's support for leaders so they can coach and develop their employees successfully.

It is through a Growth through Learning orientation at a team level that organizations can engage employees, innovate, and develop organizational resiliency and adaptability. It is through these team cultures of learning that organizations can maintain sustainable growth and extend their lifespan beyond 15 years.

A Focus on Learning

"Recently, I was asked if I was going to fire an employee who made a mistake that cost the company $600,000. 'No,' I replied, 'I just spent $600,000 training him. Why would I want somebody to hire his experience?'"

- Thomas John Watson Sr.,
Former Chair and CEO of IBM

CHAPTER 8

A Learning-Focused Workplace

An output-focused workplace is a pretty grim place. In reality, organizations are rarely, if ever, as uniform as I described. They are more like a kaleidoscope, with some teams more entrenched in an output focus than others, and with shifting extremes over time.

I have a program where leaders complete a diagnostic to identify their mindset and behaviours and the extent to which they focus on output versus learning and growth. In the workshop that follows the diagnostic, I draw the Growth through Learning model that I introduced in Chapter Three. I ask the leaders to plot where they are individually (X) and as an organization (O).

Here's an example from one leadership team:

Growth through Learning Model

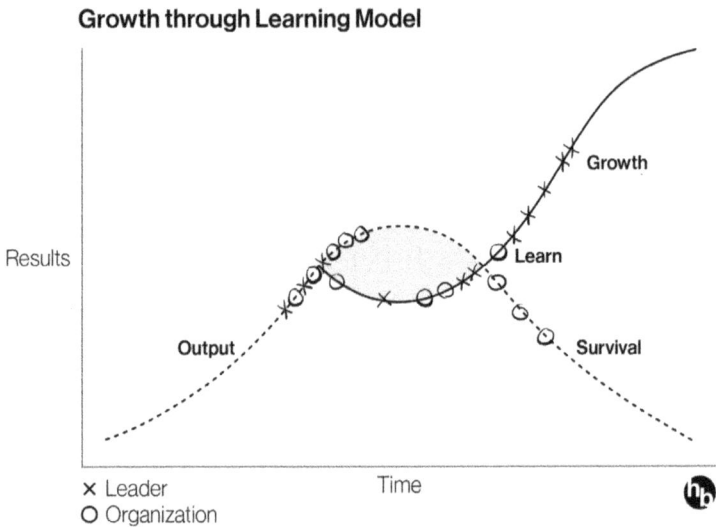

You can see there's a range where these leaders placed their organization (O). No one felt they were firmly planted in an output focus. Interestingly, some felt their organization was already slipping into survival mode. When looking at where leaders place themselves (X), you can see some are inching close to Learn, some are in the middle of it, while quite a few are progressing up the Growth curve.

This organization is in transition. A new CEO started in the past four years and they have been moving from a very established culture of getting short-term results to thinking strategically about where they are headed long term. These leaders have been stressed and are burned out. They are passionate and still committed to the purpose and vision of their organization, but they are struggling with balancing work with personal time and professional development. The organization has experienced higher turnover in recent years, which is natural when there's a change of leadership. The turnover is also because of the high-stress leaders and their employees' experience, and the lack of professional development and career growth.

Where would you plot yourself and your organization if you completed my diagnostic and workshop? Where would your fellow leaders and team members make their mark?

Moving out of an output-focused workplace requires learning. Instead of reacting in the moment and working to address immediate needs, leaders start building skills within their teams and prioritize growth through learning. Employees move from feeling stressed about their work to being committed to their leader, team, and organization.

Making this transition requires the leader to be open to new ideas, perspectives, and ways of working. If this doesn't happen and the leader resists, they and their team will slide into survival mode.

This transition isn't easy. It's not a straight, linear process, and it takes time. You briefly met Christy Billan in Chapter One, when she shared how recruiting is one of the top challenges leaders and organizations face.

Christy Billan and I also talked about her evolution as a leader and the critical shift she made from a command-and-control style to a guide-and-empower style during her leadership journey. Christy first led a team when she moved from being a team member to leading the team. As a new leader, she had high expectations of herself. She had been promoted from within the team to lead it and felt she had something to prove. She had her hands in everything, trying to control the work of her team. Because she had done the work as a team member, she remembers how easy it was to flip back into 'doing mode.' When she first started leading her team, she recalls being very explicit. "This is how it needs to be done" and, "This is what we're going to do" were common phrases she used.

Christy's micromanaging approach had unintended consequences. She remembers feeling busy and overwhelmed. She realized she was the root of the problem. What it boiled down to was that the team wasn't empowered to operate without her. They didn't have the confidence, power, or authority to make decisions. Everything had to be run through Christy, which meant she was overwhelmed and stressed and ended up being a bottleneck.

Christy's leadership journey provides a picture of a leader with an output focus who, with all good intentions, did not develop her team and increase their capability. In failing to do so, she created additional stress for herself.

Listen to my conversation with Christy in my *Growth through Learning* podcast. Go to **www.hannahbrown.co/resources/podcast** or wherever you find your podcasts.

In his book, *Transitions: Making Sense of Life's Changes,*[93] William Bridges provides an elegantly simple model for personal change – or 'transition' as he calls it. It starts with an Ending, such as being laid off, letting go of a hero identity, or shifting away from an output focus. Before we can move onto a

New Beginning, we must spend time in the Neutral Zone. I call this the 'messy middle,' which aptly describes the Learn phase of my Growth through Learning model.

William Bridges' model applies to leaders and organizations alike as they transition from an output focus to a growth focus. I can see elements of Endings, New Beginnings, and the Neutral Zone in Christy's leadership journey.

Out of an Output Focus

How do leaders and organizations move from an output focus to achieve growth? How do leaders rethink their approach to leadership the way Christy Billan did in the last chapter? Or how Christine Helgerman did in Chapter Three when she needed to recondition her staff to make decisions on their own instead of running decisions through her?

Learning is the key that unlocks this shift. There are three areas to focus on to achieve growth through learning:

- Learning Mindset
- Team Culture
- Organization Support.

The first two – Learning Mindset and Team Culture – are within the leader's scope of control. The third rests with the organization. If you are an executive, you likely have a direct influence on all three.

Let's examine each of these in detail and consider how, when combined, they move leaders and organizations from short-term results to long-term sustained growth and prepare them for a complex and changing work landscape. We'll begin with nurturing a Learning Mindset, as it is the foundation for creating a Growth through Learning orientation.

CHAPTER 9
Learning Mindset

"The ability to learn is the most
important quality a leader can have."

– Padmasree Warrior

Alearning mindset is similar to a growth mindset, which Carol Dweck defined in her book, *Mindset: The New Psychology of Success.*[94] Let me touch on her work to lay the foundation for how I define a learning mindset. Dweck outlines two mindsets: fixed and growth. People with a fixed mindset believe their talents and capabilities are inherently stable and unchangeable over time. They experience life as a series of tests that judge their innate abilities. Challenges are often avoided for fear of failure or looking inadequate, leading to a tendency to stick with what they know and avoid risks that could lead to error, embarrassment or criticism.

In contrast, people with a growth mindset believe their talents can be developed, and therefore, their capabilities are endless. They experience life as an ongoing journey of development, rich with opportunities for continuous learning. Challenges are embraced as chances to grow, and setbacks are viewed as valuable feedback. This openness fosters resilience, encourages innovation, and drives them to strive for improvement rather than shying away from difficulties.

Our mindset shows up in all facets of our lives. Summers in Ontario are fleeting; school is out, the weather is warm, and the pace slows down as people go on much-needed vacations. My family travels to 'cottage country' usually twice a summer. We head up Highway 400 to Muskoka and enjoy cottage life – reading on the dock, swimming in the lake, kayaking and feasting on great food (as an aside, much of this book was written and edited on various docks in Muskoka).

I find people are more friendly at the cottage. Boaters wave to one another when passing by and comment on the weather or the stillness of the lake. I went for a paddle at one cottage and, as expected, people on docks waved and made friendly comments. I passed one cottage where two men were relaxing on the dock. Instead of a general wave and friendly comment, one man said, "You're putting me to shame with your exercise and paddling. I'm just sitting on the dock here." I responded with a generic affirming comment so he could feel better. I realized after that his comment reflected a fixed mindset. I think, in his mind, my actions were related to his behaviour. In this situation, he fell short and inadequate. Life for him was a competition – a series of tests – where he needed to continually prove himself.

A Growth through Learning orientation requires a growth mindset that leaves us open to changing and developing. Expanding on the concept of a growth mindset, a learning mindset introduces additional factors needed for sustained learning and development. First, a learning mindset includes curiosity, which means individuals and teams continually seek new knowledge and challenge the status quo. This goes hand-in-hand with courage, essential for embracing the vulnerabilities that come with being open to new situations and ideas. Finally, being consistent in these efforts embeds these behaviours into the team's DNA, making learning an ever-present goal rather than an intermittent one. Unlike a growth mindset, which focuses on the belief in one's personal ability to develop, a learning mindset encompasses a proactive pursuit of growth that engages the individual and, by extension, the team.

Curious to explore new things

"Minds are like parachutes;
they work best when open."

- T. Dewar

Ian Leslie's book, *Curious: The Desire to Know and Why Your Future Depends on It*[95] highlights that curiosity is a fundamental part of being human. As Leslie does, you could say that curiosity is the fourth human drive after food, sex, and shelter. Curiosity moves us from being indifferent to experiences and people around us to being inquisitive. There are so many ripple effects of this. Being inquisitive or curious boosts creativity and innovation.[96] For example, in call centres, new employees who were curious asked more questions of co-workers, which provided the information they needed to perform their jobs and helped them be more creative in addressing customer concerns.[97] Cultivating curiosity helps leaders and employees adapt to uncertain market conditions and external pressures because they think more deeply and rationally about decisions and identify more creative solutions.[98]

In another study,[99] employees started their day with a text message that either prompted curiosity (e.g., What is one topic or activity you are curious about today?) or triggered reflection but not curiosity (e.g., What is one topic or activity you'll engage in today?). After four weeks, the employees who received the prompts focused on curiosity were more innovative. They made more constructive suggestions for implementing solutions to organizational problems.

As leaders, we can learn from this study and nurture curiosity in our teams. We can begin team meetings by asking what people are curious about.

My *Lead, Learn, Grow Conversation Cards* are designed for leaders to use with their teams. They include questions to promote curiosity, inspire courage, and develop consistency. Go to **www.hannahbrown.co/resources/conversation-cards** to find out more.

Focusing on curiosity helps leaders learn and future-proof their careers. Role-modeling curiosity encourages it in others, which leads to curiosity across the team.[100] In teams, curiosity improves performance because it improves communication. Being curious requires the ability to step outside of one's comfort zone and be open to other information and perspectives. This openness requires the ability to communicate.

In a study[101] of students in a leadership program at Harvard Kennedy School, researchers divided the participants into groups to complete a simulation. Some groups completed a task before the simulation to heighten their curiosity. The groups that completed the additional task performed better. The researchers attributed this higher performance to their increased curiosity, which led to improved communication – sharing information, asking questions, and listening to each other. Again, as leaders, we can encourage our teams to share information, ask questions, and listen to each other to improve our team's performance.

Curiosity increases our brain's ability to learn new information. I think of curiosity as the ingredient that turns our brains into super-sponges. Matthias Gruber is a cognitive neuroscientist who studies how curiosity affects learning. He has identified[102] that curiosity stimulates what he calls the brain's 'wanting system.' It creates a surge in dopamine, so we seek out new information. If we are even a little bit curious about something, it triggers dopamine, which makes us want more. It's the 'wanting more' that makes us ask questions and learn new things. When we seek out new information to feed that curiosity, we generate more dopamine. Curiosity and the dopamine effect also help us retain what we learn. Matthias Gruber discovered that curiosity helps turn knowledge into long-term memories we can access later.

When researching this book, I visited the nursery school my children attended as toddlers. The concept of curiosity was at the forefront of my mind, and with my teenage children beside me, I saw the toddlers playing in such a new light. They were learning how high they could jump, figuring out how to stack blocks, and making noises as toy dinosaurs navigated imaginary terrain and battled each other. We are born naturally curious and, somehow, as we grow up, we lose that natural inquisitiveness and sheer delight in the new and unexpected.

Schools and workplaces

> *"It is a miracle that curiosity survives formal education."*
>
> – Albert Einstein

Why does this decline happen? One contributing factor is the structure of our schools and workplaces. Schools place importance on test scores and grades,[103] which encourages 'performance goals' that emphasize doing well. Learning becomes a means to an end and perpetuates a fixed mindset. It sounds like, "I want to get a good grade." In contrast, 'mastery goals' emphasize understanding and lead to more self-directed and sustained learning. We learn because we want to understand and know the answer, not to get a good grade on a test. This sounds like, "I am interested in this and want to understand how it works."

The structure of our education system extends into our workplaces that prioritize output and short-term results. Test scores are replaced with objectives and performance reviews, leaving little room for 'mastery goals' and curiosity to learn. There's a disconnect in our workplaces when it comes to curiosity. On the one hand, leaders and employees agree that curiosity is good for the organization. In a survey of over 3,000 employees, 92% credited curiosity towards new ideas as a catalyst for job satisfaction, motivation, and high performance.[104] The World Economic Forum[105] lists curiosity and lifelong learning as one of the top ten in-demand job skills needed now and in the future. These skills are essential for employees adapting to change and disrupted workplaces.

Yet, leaders continue to prioritize output – getting results – over being curious about and exploring new ideas.[106] Some argue that it's harder to manage people if they are allowed to explore their own interests. Or, there could be disagreements that slow down decision-making and raise the cost of doing business. There's truth in this; exploration and curiosity involve asking questions and challenging the status quo. They also lead to more options and the possibility of a better solution.

Talk instead of listening

Another contributing factor to our declining curiosity is that we typically prefer talking instead of listening. When confronted with an organizational crisis, most high-level leaders in an executive education program said they would take action. Only a few said they would ask questions before imposing their ideas on others.[107] In *Curious: The Desire to Know and Why Your Future Depends on It*,[108] Ian Leslie says, "Questions weaponize curiosity, turning it into a tool for changing behaviour." Leslie goes on to share this example from the former Chief Executive Officer (CEO) of Dow Chemical, Mike Parker:

> *"A lot of bad leadership comes from an inability or*
> *unwillingness to ask questions. I have watched talented*
> *people – people with much higher IQs than mine – who*

have failed as leaders. They can talk brilliantly, with a great breadth of knowledge, but they're not very good at asking questions. So while they know a lot at a high level, they don't know what's going on way down in the system. Sometimes they are afraid of asking questions, but what they don't realize is that the dumbest questions can be very powerful. They can unlock a conversation."

We need to be curious to ask questions. As Mike Parker points out, we also need the courage to admit we don't know the answer. Finally, we need the willingness to listen to the answer, and the openness to consider new information and perspectives.

Surprise and knowledge

Our openness to the unexpected also impacts our level of curiosity. Our curiosity is at its greatest when there is an element of surprise. There needs to be a bit of surprise or uncertainty, but not too much. A teacher showing a box and saying, "This is a box. It's a rectangle." doesn't elicit any surprise or stimulate curiosity. If, instead, the teacher says, "This is a box. It's a rectangle. What do you think is inside this box?" there's an element of surprise or uncertainty. Right away, there's a higher level of curiosity, which triggers dopamine to make us want to learn more and helps encode our new knowledge into long-term memory.

However, if there is too much surprise or uncertainty, it can be overwhelming. We become fearful or anxious, and our curiosity shuts off. As leaders, we can ask questions to encourage curiosity. We can also present information with elements of the unknown. We don't need to have all the answers. In fact, when we don't, there's room for our teams to participate in gathering information and determining the best path forward. It heightens their curiosity and engages them in the process.

A leader with a hero identity feels compelled to have all the answers. A leader with a coaching identity knows there's value in the unknown and that there's benefit in asking questions instead of providing solutions. Leaders who demonstrate vulnerability by not providing all the answers increase trust on their teams and create a safe space for learning and growth.[109]

Finally, our life experience contributes to our declining curiosity. In addition to surprise, curiosity is at its greatest when we have baseline knowledge, but not so much that we feel like we've mastered the topic.[110] To be curious about something, you need to know at least a little bit about it. For example, to be curious about semiconductor chip manufacturing, I would need to know at least something about it. If I knew absolutely nothing, I wouldn't even know it existed and wouldn't have any questions to ask to feed my curiosity. Likewise, if I knew a tremendous amount about semiconductor chip manufacturing, I might not be curious because I might feel like I already know everything. To be curious, I need to know a little bit, but not too much. Research supports this and shows that at work, our curiosity declines the longer we're in our job.[111] We learn how to perform well in our job and, without new experiences, we can stagnate.

Staying curious

While curiosity is a central part of being human, and we pursue it naturally as children, many of us lose our curiosity as we grow up and enter the workforce. We need to nurture curiosity in ourselves and as leaders in our teams. As Ian Leslie[112] wrote,

"The flame of curiosity doesn't burn in a vacuum."

- Ian Leslie

We learn and gain life experiences as we age. Over time, we may become complacent and become less curious to learn new things or try new experiences. Applied to a work context, the longer we have been in the workforce or in our role, the more confidence we may have in our knowledge and expertise. The risk is that this causes complacency and decreased curiosity as we feel we know everything. We can become indifferent instead of inquisitive. While this can happen, it doesn't have to. Our brains are incredible organs capable of learning, regardless of our age.[113] Neuroplasticity is the brain's ability to change and adapt based on our experiences. The study of neuroplasticity originated with research into brain trauma, but in more recent years, it has expanded to provide insights into adult learning.

When we're born, we have a set number of neurons that communicate with each other, sharing information through synapses. When we learn, we strengthen these synapses and rewire the neural connections. This creates new memories and connections between existing information. This rewiring continues throughout our lifetime.

Our brains can also grow new neurons in one specific area of the brain – the hippocampus. This is the area of the brain responsible for creating memories, including spatial memory and navigation. We know this because when someone's hippocampus is damaged, they have amnesia. An interesting study[114] of licenced taxi drivers in London revealed that they have larger hippocampi than people who don't drive taxis. The researchers concluded that the taxi drivers' hippocampi developed additional neurons and grew as they learned all of London's streets and how to navigate them. So we can grow new neurons and learn new things as we age!

Complacency, decreased curiosity and less learning are not inevitable. Our brains can keep learning. It's up to us to choose learning and nurture a learning mindset.

What are you curious about? Where can you continue to learn and grow as an individual and as a leader?

Courage to take risks

"Don't be afraid to fail. Be afraid not to try."

– Michael Jordan

The second factor to focus on when nurturing a learning mindset is courage – emotional and social courage. It takes courage to try new things and experiment, knowing you might make a mistake or fail.

In my early twenties, I lived in downtown Toronto. I was single, lived on my own and was discovering my way in the world. There was this one building that I lived close to and often walked by. The large windows were always steamed up, so much so that I couldn't see what was happening inside. I became curious. Eventually, I went in, discovered it was a karate dojo, and decided to join. Karate became a passion of mine at that time in my life. I got in shape and discovered a sense of community and purpose in a large city. I developed goals and gained a sense of accomplishment as I moved from white to yellow to blue belt (no, I didn't get my black belt). It wasn't easy at the beginning. The dojo had mirrors alongside one wall so we could see our form, stance, and movements. We could see each misstep – there was no hiding! I remember thinking how awkward I felt and looked. I made many mistakes as I learned. I couldn't remember the last time I had learned something new that was physical – maybe golf lessons a

few years prior, or learning to ride a bike as a kid. It took
courage for me to go into the dojo, sign up, and learn a
new skill. Learning is hard, and sometimes that difficulty
and the fear of failure means we never make that first step
and try.

In Chapter Two, you met Julianna Morris, who heads up Porsche People Excellence in Training at Porsche Cars Canada. In addition to talking about formal training programs, we discussed the courage it takes to learn new things.

Julianna describes herself as a person with lifelong
curiosity. She wants to understand why things happen
and how they work. "When I see something that someone
has done really well, I want to find out. What did you do?
How did you do it? And what did it take for you to develop
that way?"
Julianna used the word 'playful' to describe her curiosity
and approach to learning. When playful, we aren't afraid
to fail. "Most of the time, we don't try something because of
fear of looking like we don't know what we're doing. And
looking like, you know, you've messed up. No one wants
that. No one wants to look like they've messed up something
or didn't do it successfully. So I think removing the fear
allows you to just say 'hey, at least I tried!' We need to
give ourselves permission to fail and be okay with that. We
aren't perfect, and learning something new is important."

I love Julianna's approach to learning and taking risks. I think 'playful' is a great way to embrace the courage it takes to learn new things. Kids are natural at playing, and they learn from mistakes all the time. As adults, when we can tap into our playful side, we can embrace a lighter approach to learning new things.

Listen to my conversation with Julianna in my *Growth through Learning* podcast. Go to **www.hannahbrown.co/resources/podcast** or wherever you find your podcasts.

Dave Stachowiak has been hosting the podcast *Coaching for Leaders* since 2011. In episode 464, his guest Jonathan Raymond shared:

*"You don't get to look good
and grow at the same time."*

- Jonathan Raymond

I love this quote and have it on a sticky note beside my computer monitor as a reminder that learning takes courage and I may not always be successful at first. I share it with you because, as leaders, we have an important role in creating a safe physical and emotional environment for our teams.

If we've met in person, you would probably know that I have a fairly loud voice. This served me well when I was a teenager and teaching swimming lessons. I could holler across the pool, and the little swimmers could easily hear me. It didn't serve me so well when I was in elementary school. I decided to join the Glee Club sometime between grades two and five. I went to a really old school that didn't have a gym with a stage for concerts. Instead, my school had this big staircase that came down to a central hallway. We would line up on the steps to create a choir. I can remember singing away to my heart's content during practice. The teacher, whose name I still remember but won't share so she can remain anonymous, came up to me and suggested that I sing in my whisper voice. I was absolutely crushed. To this day, I do not sing in public – actually, I don't really sing at all. The message I received was that she didn't want to hear what I had to say – I didn't have a voice.

I share this experience because, as an adult now, it makes me think of vulnerability and psychological safety. We didn't have the term back then, but that doesn't mean it didn't exist. As leaders, it's so important to be aware of the words you use and the impact they can have. Leaders need to be conscious of creating a safe space for employees to have a voice and speak up, even if they're loud and a little off-key. I don't think my teacher knew how her words impacted me. I didn't have the courage to speak up and say something.

What are examples from your life where you struggled to find courage – when you didn't feel safe or have a voice? How has that shaped you as a person and as a leader? In what ways might you be like my teacher and, unknowingly, creating a space where your employees feel shut down or like they can't speak up?

Psychological safety

There are two pillars that underpin courage in nurturing a Learning Mindset. The first is psychological safety. It's critical in empowering employees to 'have a voice.' It helps people speak up, share ideas, and ask questions.[115] Psychological safety helps people feel secure and capable of change.[116] It also helps employees overcome feeling defensive or anxious at work so they can focus on solving problems and achieving shared goals.[117] Finally, when employees feel psychologically safe at work, they are more engaged and have higher job satisfaction.[118]

Leaders are the central figures in creating a climate of psychological safety for their employees.[119] Since Amy Edmondson coined the term psychological safety and wrote the book, *The Fearless Organization: Creating Psychological Safety in the Workplace for Learning, Innovation, and Growth,*[120] there has been a plethora of research on team and individual psychological safety. Amy Edmonson and Derrick Bransby completed a thorough literature review and analyzed the findings from the past ten years.[121] The research continues to identify leaders' significant role in creating psychological safety. They identify three overarching leadership attributes that can enhance or weaken team psychological safety:

- Listening – When leaders listen to their employees (truly listen, with their full attention), they increase the level of psychological safety.[122]
- Competence – When leaders demonstrate they are capable in their job, the psychological safety in their team increases.[123]

- Transparency – When leaders share relevant information, are open to feedback, and are forthcoming about motives and reasons behind decisions, psychological safety increases.[124]

I want to expand on competence because, on the surface, it could seem to contradict what I wrote earlier about leaders needing to let go of expert and hero identities. It raises the question, "How can a leader be competent if they're not the expert?" Competence for a leader isn't as much about knowing the technical details of their team members' work as it is about being competent as a leader. Imagine a sea-faring vessel with a captain and crew. When the captain sets the direction and uses the compass, map, and other instruments to chart the course, the crew is confident in the captain's ability and can focus on their tasks. The captain's competence isn't in the rigging but in setting the direction. So, too, leaders in organizations need to focus on the objectives, setting the plan and guiding the direction, not getting involved in the rigging.

Vulnerability

Vulnerability is the second pillar underpinning courage in a Learning Mindset. Brené Brown defines vulnerability as "Uncertainty, risk, and emotional exposure."[125] There is vulnerability in learning because when we learn, we are exposed to new ideas, concepts, and perspectives that might be contrary to what we already believe. If we aren't uncomfortable, we aren't being challenged.

As leaders, being vulnerable means we show up and are seen even when there are no guarantees of success. In this light, vulnerability is the most accurate measure of courage. Brené Brown connects vulnerability to innovation, and states,

---

*"Vulnerability is the birthplace
of creativity and courage."*

- Brené Brown

When leaders embrace their vulnerability and role model courage, they create an environment where employees can experiment, take risks, and learn from failure. Employees on these teams are five times more likely to trust their leaders.[126] Furthermore, when leaders acknowledge their shortcomings or failures, they are seven times more likely to maintain trust over leaders who don't demonstrate this type of vulnerability.[127] These teams are nearly three times more likely to develop new ideas or solutions than 'low trust' teams[128] because team members are less concerned with failing and instead see new ideas as opportunities to learn.

In Chapter One, I introduced Adam Stephens, the director of Marketing and Community Engagement at The Humane Society of Kitchener Waterloo & Stratford Perth. In addition to discussing the changing social contract, we also discussed role-modelling vulnerability and creating more personal relationships at work.

Adam and I talked about what prevents leaders from taking a more empathetic, human approach to leadership. He shared that leaders are often insecure and afraid of failure. He gave the example of a new manager whom he had just promoted. This new manager was portraying an overly professional, impersonal image with his team, which Adam could see wasn't resonating with the team members. Through conversations with the new manager, Adam realized the new manager was insecure and afraid of letting his personal side show. To coach this new manager and role model how to be more personal, Adam invited him to department meetings to observe his leadership style. Adam made a point of demonstrating vulnerability. He wanted his new manager to see what vulnerability looked like and observe the positive reaction from others. Adam then worked with his new manager to identify how he could incorporate a more authentic and caring approach to his leadership.

Listen to my conversation with Adam in my *Growth through Learning* podcast. Go to **www.hannahbrown.co/resources/podcast** or wherever you find your podcasts.

Psychological safety and vulnerability are two pillars that help us and our teams be courageous. Through them, we find the strength to face uncertainties head-on, embrace our imperfections as opportunities for growth, and share our experiences – both triumphs and setbacks – with authenticity.

There is so much research and support for the benefits of being courageous at work. And yet, it is incredibly difficult to do. I see courage as a series of ongoing small acts instead of a few large gestures. As individuals, it's the willingness to try something new – go into a karate dojo or offer an alternative perspective in a team meeting. It means choosing to view failures as opportunities to learn and not being overly self-critical when things go wrong. As leaders, courage means role modelling, being vulnerable and creating a space where team members feel safe to express themselves, be authentic, and, if needed, sing a little bit off-key.

When we embrace courage, we move from being fearful to being confidently vulnerable. Our teams become more creative, innovative, and a joy to be a part of.

Consistently learning

"Motivation is what gets you started.
Habit is what keeps you going."

– Jim Ryun

I'm really good at generating ideas and starting new things. I'm terrible at following through and implementing those ideas. In my personal life, my husband often steps in to make sure an idea or new action 'grows legs' and becomes part of our family practices (Dave wants to add that sometimes I start more things than he's comfortable with!). At work, I delegate to people who see my ideas through to implementation. When it comes to individual learning and being consistent, there's no husband and no administrative support. It's all on us!

Having a Learning Mindset means learning is integrated into our lives. It's more than taking a training course or obtaining an MBA. It's part of who we are as individuals and as leaders. A

Learning Mindset requires consistency – a habit of learning so we continue to learn and grow throughout our lives. We know our brains can continue to learn; it's up to us to continuously choose to be curious and courageous.

It is hard, though, and I can attest that it's tough to do consistently. So, what's the benefit of trying?

When we develop a habit of learning, we lay a foundation for a healthy mental life in the future. In 2013, a research study explored the effects of old age on the brain's cognitive decline.[129] Wilson and his team discovered that engaging in cognitively demanding activities such as reading and writing as a lifelong habit (from childhood through to old age) slowed the rate of mental decline by a third compared to those who did an average amount of cognitively demanding activities. Furthermore, people who rarely read or wrote experienced a mental decline 48% faster than the average participants in the study.

Teams benefit from leaders who have a Learning Mindset, because it becomes a part of their culture. When people feel psychologically safe, learning behaviours are fostered through transferring and sharing knowledge, by speaking up with new ideas, and through an atmosphere of creativity.[130]

When teams adopt a Learning Mindset, their workplace becomes a safe space for exploring ideas and having open communication. These concepts are rooted in Amy Edmondson's research on psychological safety and in her book, *The Fearless Organization: Creating Psychological Safety in the Workplace for Learning, Innovation, and Growth.* Secure in their ability to freely express thoughts and ideas, team members engage in richer collaboration and gain a deeper understanding of complex challenges. This engagement fosters creativity and resilience, turning groups of individuals into teams of innovation that are more capable of solving problems.[131]

Aside from what the research says, haven't you found that teams you've been on are more enjoyable when you trust each other? I remember the team I was on when I was the director of sales training for North America at a life insurance company years ago. We were candid with each other, felt like we 'had each other's backs' and could push each other to try new things and test out new ideas. I am still in touch with some of these colleagues even though it's been 20 years since we worked together!

A habit of learning with individuals and teams also benefits organizations. A culture of learning leads to continuous improvement, helps retain talented workers, increases collaboration, and extends the longevity of the business.[132] I've been working with the leadership team of a medium-sized non-profit in the technology space. They wanted to address employee turnover and, as a smaller organization, identify how to provide development opportunities to employees given their flat organizational structure. The leadership team completed my diagnostic to assess their comfort and effectiveness with Learning Mindset and Team Culture and to provide feedback on the Organization Support they received. The diagnostic identified Learning Mindset overall and coaching specifically as the greatest opportunities to focus on. In a post-workshop impact session, the CEO shared his vision for leaders coaching and supporting employees on their teams and, more broadly, across the organization. He wanted them to lead with learning to break down silos in the organization. He wanted leaders to coach employees on their own teams and in other teams to reduce division in the organization. Through this cross-coaching approach, leaders and employees learn about work in other departments across the organization. The CEO's focus on coaching and cross-team coaching prioritizes growth through learning and identifies coaching as the consistent practice to make it happen.

Creating habits

It's one thing to recognize and even believe in the benefits of learning; it's another to put it into action. You may be like me and struggle to implement ideas on an ongoing basis. One of the barriers I often hear from individuals and leaders alike is lack of time. Earlier, I shared my perspective on time and reframed it as a prioritization challenge. Reprioritizing is one way to unlock the time conundrum. Another is establishing habits. Developing consistency around learning and embedding it into who we are as leaders and in the culture of our teams requires habit. As Charles Duhigg[133] writes in his book, *The Power of Habit: Why we do what we do in life and business,*

"40% of the actions people perform each day aren't actual decisions."

– Charles Duhigg

Habits emerge because our brains are constantly looking for ways to conserve energy. Once a habit is established – like having a drink after work or looking to the leader to start team meetings – the brain stops participating in decision-making. It doesn't have to work hard and determine how to unwind after work or read the room to figure out who will talk first. The brain can divert energy to other tasks.

I've loved travelling since I went on a six-week exchange program to mainland China as a teenager. I was 18 years old and China was just opening up to the West. It was a pretty memorable experience. Since then, I've noticed that travelling is tiring. I think this is because we have so few habits when we travel. Basic things like making coffee or deciding what to eat for breakfast are all new. At home, in our familiar environments, these activities are automatic, so we don't need to spend mental energy on them. When travelling, these basic activities, while joyful, take up mental energy. It's part of the experience and the adventure and why we learn when we travel. It's also why we often feel like we need a vacation from our vacation when we're back at home.

Just like when we travel, trying new things at work takes mental energy. By making learning a habit, we decrease the mental energy it requires.

Charles Duhigg explains that at a high level, a habit is a three-step loop:

- A cue or trigger that tells your brain to go into automatic mode
- An automatic behaviour or action
- A reward, which further embeds the behaviour as a habit.

Here's an example. Several months ago, I started keeping a five-year journal. I leave it on my bedside table or even on my pillow so I remember to write in it. Before bed, I jot down three points about the day. I focus on gratitude and accomplishments. The trigger is the book by my bed. The action is writing – it's short, so I've been able to maintain it. The reward is moving the string bookmark and seeing all the pages I've completed. I anticipate the sense of accomplishment of maintaining this habit and observing what I've learned and how I've grown over the years.

You may be thinking, "Yes, this is great in theory, but I'm terrible at developing and keeping habits." You're not alone! One trick is to 'stack your habits.'[134] As James Clear references in his book, *Atomic Habits: An Easy & Proven Way to Build Good Habits & Break Bad Ones*, instead of pairing a new habit with a time or location, pair it with a current habit. Here's Clear's formula:

"After/Before [current habit], I will [new habit]."

Over the summer writing and editing this book, I developed this habit:

When I wake up, I make a tea [current habit],
go to the back deck or dock, and write [new habit].

This new habit became firmly embedded. By the time you're reading this, hopefully, I will have tweaked this established, stacked habit into something new that still includes my morning tea and time to write.

Habit stacking works well because our existing habits are so entrenched. As you think about how you want to nurture your Learning Mindset, consider the things you already do and find ways to incorporate learning into your existing habits. As a habit, learning will become integrated into your day, meaning it will take up less brain energy to do it.

A Learning Mindset includes tapping into and nurturing our curiosity, which leads to creativity and innovation. It also requires having the courage to follow our curiosity, take risks, and experiment, even if we might fail. It is often in making mistakes that we find our greatest growth. Finally, to fully embrace a Learning Mindset, we need to develop habits for consistency, so our learning and growth is part of who we are as individuals and as leaders.

Team Culture is the next area of focus to develop a Growth through Learning orientation and move from Output to Growth. This is where we use the Learning Mindset we've nurtured in ourselves and extend it to others through the Team Culture we create.

CHAPTER 10

Team Culture

"If you want to go fast, go alone.
If you want to go far, go together."

– African proverb

Reflecting back, you'll remember there are three areas to focus on to achieve a Growth through Learning orientation:

- Learning Mindset
- Team Culture
- Organization Support

Team Culture is the second area to focus on when moving from an output to a growth-focused workplace. This shift enables us to respond to changing demographics, skills shortages, and technological disruptions. If you are a leader in a functional area and have direct reports, you may find that Learning

Mindset and Team Culture are what provide the most value of the three areas of focus above.

Culture can feel a bit nebulous – vague and difficult to define. If we consider it at face value, as a word in our vocabulary, the Merriam-Webster[135] dictionary defines culture in a few ways:

- The customary beliefs, social norms, and material traits of a racial, religious, or social group.
- The set of shared attitudes, values, goals, and practices that characterizes an institution or organization.
- The integrated pattern of human knowledge, belief, and behaviour that depends upon the capacity for learning and transmitting knowledge to succeeding generations.

In the context of teams and organizations, I like the simple definition offered by Gallup:[136] "How we do things around here."

Beyond this definition, what makes a great culture? Daniel Coyle[137] identifies three characteristics of a great Team Culture.

- Build safety – establish a deep sense of belonging to the group, connection between team members, and psychological safety.
- Share vulnerability – practise being vulnerable to build trust and encourage open communication.
- Establish purpose – create a shared purpose and vision the team can rally behind.

Applied to a Growth through Learning orientation, the first two characteristics – build safety and share vulnerability – are both central to nurturing a Learning Mindset. Establishing purpose is central to shifting from an output-focused workplace to a growth-focused workplace where learning and employee growth are prioritized alongside achieving results.

I want to expand on Coyle's work on culture with my 20+ years in training and development to bring a learning lens to culture. To create a Team Culture of learning, leaders need to embrace three practices. They need to commit to developing their employees alongside getting results. They need to care for their employees as human beings beyond the work they do, and who they are as people. And, finally, leaders need to embrace a coach-like approach to leadership. Let's look at each of these in turn.

Commitment to change

---

*"Commitment is what transforms
a promise into reality."*

– Abraham Lincoln

Moving from an output to a growth focus that prioritizes coaching and developing employees can feel like a gargantuan task. Again, I think of all the leaders I work with who struggle with a lack of time and ask, "How is it even possible to do more on top of what I'm already doing?" There needs to be a commitment to change – to lead differently.

> *I've worked with Shaun Scott, the director of Human Resources at Linamar Corporation, since 2012, when we created and started facilitating Linamar's Business Leadership program. It supports senior leaders in developing financial acumen and negotiation skills and stretches them to think more strategically. Shaun and I met for lunch in the early days of planning and researching this book. He shared an interesting perspective: for leaders to change how they lead, they need to be uncomfortable with the status quo.*

If a leader is struggling and focused on output, they are probably dealing with employee disengagement and turnover. For this to be a catalyst for change and a new leadership approach, the discomfort of constantly recruiting, hiring, and onboarding new employees needs to be greater than the discomfort of changing.

The catalyst for change can also come from a personal experience. In Chapter Five, I introduced Janice and her experience with the struggling product launch in India.

> *Janice and I also talked about her transition into the leader she is today. She had a catalyst moment that helped her overcome her imposter syndrome, gain confidence in her leadership style, and learn about herself so she could be a better leader.*

> *Janice was working for a different tech company that went under in the wake of the 2008 US housing market collapse and the Great Recession. The company folded, and she found herself without a job. She picked up her four-year-old child from school that day and explained how she didn't have a job anymore and would be at home more. Her child responded, "Now you can finally spend time with me!" What a shock to hear the truth spoken so plainly! Janice spent time over the next several months reflecting on her child's response and on the type of parent, leader, and person she was.*

Janice's continued story outlines the catalyst that caused her to reflect on who she wanted to be. After playing through scenarios and having grandiose thoughts of how, if she had worked better, differently, harder, the company wouldn't have folded, she realized the type of leader she wanted to be. Fast forward to today, and her LinkedIn profile has the tagline, "Leader with a learning mindset." Beautiful!

Finally, many leaders are prompted to change because of feedback they received in a 360-degree review. Leaders who choose to accept this honest, yet often critical feedback as a gift instead of dismissing it have an opportunity to refocus their leadership approach.

You met Christy Billan, director of Small Business Lending Products at Farm Credit Canada (FCC), in Chapter One and again a few chapters ago. Let's continue to follow her journey as a leader and look at what prompted her to move away from trying to control everything, feeling overwhelmed, and having no capacity.

I asked Christy what the catalyst was for her to shift her leadership approach. She said her high stress level and capacity constraints caused her to do some soul-searching. She analyzed how she was spending her time and realized how often she was stepping in to do her team's work, solving their problems, and involving herself in situations that weren't related to her. Christy shared that on any given day she "was on three or four different calls trying to solve problems for my people, which, #1, took away the opportunity for them to learn how to have a difficult conversation, and #2, I'm having conversations about something that wasn't my issue and really doesn't fit into our organization's culture around taking ownership and accountability." By stepping in to do her team's work, she took away their opportunity to learn how to have difficult conversations. Ironically, ownership and accountability were pillars of her organization's culture. In trying to help her colleagues, she was leading counter to the organization.

Christy realized she couldn't continue leading in this way – she couldn't continue being the hero who solved other people's problems. She asked herself tough questions like, "Why am I working this way?" and "What's getting in my way?"

In her soul-searching, Christy considered her motivation and identity. She described 'filling her cup' as a metaphor for the reward and sense of accomplishment she felt when she solved problems for her team and got her hands deep into the work. She needed a different way to feel fulfilled. "Instead of making that call, escalating that issue on their behalf. [Instead of] feeling like I was the hero today; this is awesome. Instead, I had a coaching conversation with an employee who now feels empowered to have a good difficult conversation with their colleague and feeling really good about that." Christy redefined her sense of accomplishment from her actions in solving problems to being rewarded through the actions of her team.

Christy's story illustrates her transition as she took ownership of her role to coach and develop her employees. She examined the type of leader she wanted to be – what would 'fill her cup' – and created space for learning and coaching. In doing so, she prioritized growth through learning. She built a team with increased capacity, elevated her leadership ability, and created stability for her organization. By developing her team, she has a built-in succession plan. There's a capable team member who can step into her role when she moves on to her next adventure.

Listen to my conversation with Christy in my *Growth through Learning* podcast. Go to **www.hannahbrown.co/resources/podcast** or wherever you find your podcasts.

Change formula

Once a leader commits to leading differently, they need support to change. In their book, *The 15 Commitments of Conscious Leadership: A New Paradigm for Sustainable Success,*[138] authors Jim Dethmer, Diana Chapman, and Kaley Klemp introduce a Change Formula. It's tucked away in the back, but I think it's brilliant. I'm including it here as a model for leaders to embrace change and commit to moving beyond a focus on output and towards developing employees alongside achieving results.

Change Formula

$$(V \times D) + FS > R = C$$

Here's what the formula stands for:

- V = Vision
- D = Discomfort
- FS = First Steps
- R = Resistance
- C = Change

DISCOMFORT AND VISION

I love this model because it emphasizes the importance of discomfort with the status quo. But, as the formula above outlines, even when a leader is uncomfortable with the status quo, they need to also have a clear vision of the alternative. If you struggle with finding an alternative vision for your team, let me offer the Growth through Learning orientation as a new vision. Use this book and, more specifically, the next section – A Focus on Growth – to create a vision unique to your leadership and the Team Culture you want to create.

Working with a coach often helps leaders define a vision for their team. I am certified in the Integral Method of Coaching[139] and bring that distinct approach when I coach executives and leaders. I help leaders with a specific change they want to make and use metaphors to paint a picture and bring the leader's current situation to life. By using a robust metaphor, I find leaders are more open to and able to explore the nuances of their behaviours. They have more objectivity and can accept how they contribute to their challenges. After we agree on a metaphor for how the leader currently operates, they ask, "What's the alternative?" I create a metaphor for their future self; a vision that describes an alternative approach to their leadership. By using metaphors, we bring clarity to something nebulous and identify concrete actions in our coaching engagement. The leader then takes steps to shift from where they are currently to this new way of leading.

FIRST STEPS

Together, discomfort and vision are what motivate us to change. They are multipliers, and, like a mathematical equation, if one is zero, there is no motivation. First steps are additive; they supplement vision and discomfort and set the course of action once we're motivated to change. Together, vision, discomfort, and first steps need to be greater than our resistance for change to occur.

RESISTANCE AND CHANGE

In practical terms, this formula means that it's not enough for leaders to attend a training course on change because a course is only a first step. Without discomfort with the status quo and a vision, the motivation and commitment will be less than the resistance to change, and change will not occur. The short-term, easier path of maintaining the status quo will win out every time.

> *Sergio[x] is the HR director at a national manufacturing company. They have an established program for*

(x)   Name has been changed to maintain anonymity.

high-potential employees that has future leaders rotate through different functional areas to learn all aspects of the business, from machining in operations to marketing and finance. This rotation can last up to three years, so it's a significant investment for the employee, the organization and the leader who recommends the employee for the program. Upon completion, the employees move into senior leadership roles in the company.

Sergio shared a conversation he had with an engineering manager in one of their facilities. The manager said that he hoped his bright, capable engineer was accepted into the program because he wanted her to learn about production. Sergio asked the manager what he would do if she weren't accepted. The manager responded that he'd keep her where he was and continue on.

Sergio pointed out that every day, the engineering manager had lunch with the production manager. If the employee wasn't accepted into the program, couldn't they create an arrangement for a secondment or something on their own? The employee could still gain the production experience she needed. The engineering manager wasn't interested because it would take too much effort to coordinate the details, and he would struggle when the top engineer on his team would be in a new team in production.

This leader wants his employee to grow and develop, but isn't personally committed to the change. If we apply the change formula to this leader, his resistance – the time it would take to set up an individual secondment and personally coach and develop his employee – is greater than his motivation for his employee to grow and develop. While he is taking a first step – looking to Human Resources to develop his employee – he doesn't have enough discomfort to overcome his resistance.

There is one final point I want to make about leadership commitment. Fundamentally, leaders need to want to lead others. A promotion into the role may garner a higher salary or more vacation. It may come with prestige and a sense of power. But the person must want to lead others.

I introduced Dennis in Chapter Five, where it took him several months to learn how to delegate to his team so he could stop doing and start leading.

> *Dennis works for an international technology company. Through years of developing his sales effectiveness and deepening his knowledge of his company's products and solutions, he advanced in increasingly senior technical leadership roles. In 2022, he was asked to take on a management role and lead a team of about seven employees around the globe. Dennis hesitated to take on this new responsibility, recognizing that leading others would be quite different than being a technical leader in his field. He started in his new role in early 2023 and struggled for the first several months. He continued to step into the 'doing' aspect of his work – areas where he excelled – instead of delegating to others. Over time, he learned how to assign tasks to employees and that his role was to 'get work done through others.'*
>
> *Over his career, Dennis benefited from good managers who took care in getting to know him as a person, to understand how he worked and therefore how best to manage*

and guide him in advancing his career. In turn, Dennis emulated the management approach he received and had weekly one-on-one meetings with each of his employees and held weekly team meetings with the group. He developed positive personal relationships with his team members and, over time, learned about them beyond just their professional selves. However, in the end, Dennis realized that he just didn't like leading others. Yes, he had learned to be effective - he was a good listener and supported his employees. But he didn't prioritize building relationships and developing others. He didn't have a natural comfort with the messiness of human interaction and interpersonal dynamics. He realized his passion was with technical expertise and leading project teams instead of managing people. At the end of 2023, Dennis shared his intent to leave his management role and look for a non-management position again. Dennis is now happily self-demoted and excelling as a senior technical leader.

Many of us might be like Dennis and not want to take on the responsibility of leading a team. There is courage in identifying where your passions lie and where you can best apply your strengths. Like my friend and colleague, Matt Church,[140] I believe leadership is a decision, not a position. We can all be leaders, and we can choose whether or not that includes leading a team.

Care on a human level

*"A leader is someone willing to give [their] strength
to others that they may have the strength
to stand on their own."*

– Beth Revis

We need more care and compassion in our workplaces, not less. Caring for our employees is at the heart of creating a supportive environment that's conducive to learning, developing, and growing. Caring for employees means getting to know them as people and learning about who they are at work – what motivates them, the tasks they're most naturally skilled at, what new skills they want to develop, and what they're insecure about.

Edgar and Peter Schein were guests in episode 539 of Dave Stachowiak's podcast, *Coaching for Leaders*.[141] Building on their book, *Humble Inquiry: The Gentle Art of Asking Instead of Telling, 2nd Edition*,[142] Edgar, Peter, and Dave, discussed different levels of professional relationships, including transactional and personal.

- Level 1: Transactional relationships are characterized by maintaining professional distance. Leaders and team members interact according to their roles and maintain appropriate emotional distance. Though widely considered appropriate for organizations, this fosters low trust and communication because of individualism and competitiveness.

- Level 2: Personal relationships are characterized by openness and trust. They're based on a mutual interest in getting to know each other as 'total human beings' rather than just in our formal roles. This is the type of relationship leaders need to develop with their people.

Edgar and Peter share that to move from Level 1 to Level 2, leaders need to abandon the 'heroic leader myth.' The 'I alone' leader runs the risk of being starved of information, leading to an inability to keep up with the pace of change.[143] Leaders need to embrace their vulnerability, ask questions instead of providing directives, and build close relationships to create more open, trusting bonds that improve resiliency and the flow of information. Edgar and Peter's 'heroic leader myth' closely mirrors my 'hero identity' and incorporates a relational element. When acting the hero, leaders maintain a professional distance.

Earlier, I shared Dennis' experience with managing a team. He worked hard to be the type of leader he believed his team needed. He changed from doing the work to leading others and learned how to step back and focus on more strategic initiatives instead of getting into the weeds of operational tasks. Despite his efforts, Dennis realized he wasn't a good fit for management. He saw the importance of developing personal relationships but was more comfortable with transactional interactions that he could nurture with peers and in leading project teams. He didn't use that language, of course, but knew he was more comfortable leading project teams where conversations remained more task-focused and there was more personal distance in his

work relationships. Now, back in a technical leadership
role, he is much happier.

Developing more personal work relationships – Level 2,
as Schein and Schein describe – requires courage and vulnerability. Leaders need to be curious and have empathy for their
team members. In short, having this type of work relationship
and embracing the messiness of human emotions requires emotional intelligence.

Emotional intelligence

"You can't move up in the staircase of leadership
unless you are emotionally intelligent."

– Amit Ray

Emotional intelligence is the ability to manage our emotions and understand the emotions of the people around us.
It includes self and social awareness, and self and relationship
management. The term 'Emotional Intelligence' was coined in
1990 in a research paper by Peter Salovey and John D. Mayer.[144]
They defined it as "The ability to perceive and express emotion, assimilate emotion and thought, understand and reason
with emotion, and regulate emotion in the self and others."[145]
Through Daniel Goleman's book, *Emotional Intelligence: Why It
Can Matter More than IQ,*[146] emotional intelligence rose to our
collective awareness and is now identified as a critical leadership attribute.

We know that high emotional intelligence contributes to

individual, leader, and team effectiveness. As individuals, when we have high emotional intelligence, we empathize with others and communicate more effectively.[147,148] This helps us develop supportive and cohesive relationships at work[149] and better manage work pressures and demands.[150] From an organization's perspective, high emotional intelligence is associated with individual innovation, innovative environments, and overall higher performance.[151]

Any leader knows that leading others is an emotional endeavour. Research has shown that effective leadership depends on leaders' ability to manage their emotions proactively and reactively.[152] When leaders have high emotional intelligence and manage their emotions, they have higher individual performance[153,154] and achieve better business results.[155] Developing emotional intelligence is critical as leaders move into more senior positions.[156]

In Chapter Five, you met Olive, the corporate controller at a medium-sized food and beverage manufacturer. She shared how she prioritizes spending time with her team even though, like all of us, she's pressed for time.

Olive struggled initially in her leadership role to connect with her team. She maintained a professional, formal relationship that made it difficult.

She now leads her team with a more personal, empathetic approach. Even though this takes time in her day and takes up her mental energy, she knows a more caring approach to leadership is important. She values learning in herself and in others, and finds she also grows when she's coaching her team members.

The research is conclusive that emotional and social skills are essential for effective leadership.[157] This just makes sense. We can all think of leaders we've worked with who inspired and motivated us (and those who didn't). When we were inspired, we felt connected to a bigger purpose and like we 'mattered.' These leaders listened to us and connected with us personally – we had a relationship with them.

Emotional intelligence also impacts team performance. Leaders directly influence their employees, so their degree of emotional intelligence influences the development of the group.[158] When leaders have high emotional intelligence, the group's norms reflect a high level of shared emotional intelligence. In addition to shaping the group's norms, emotional intelligence is essential for effective team interactions and productivity. Working with others in a team is fundamentally a social activity. It can get 'messy,' so recognizing and managing emotions is critical for employees and teams.[159,160] It helps teams manage their conflict.[161] Teams with less emotional intelligence have greater and more intense conflict around both their tasks and relationships.[162] Employees on these teams have higher levels of burnout and, ultimately, less commitment to the group.[163] When teamwork gets 'messy' and people feel stressed, the leader's level of emotional intelligence strongly impacts the team's well-being[164] and the degree to which team members can work through their conflicts, decrease stress, and increase their commitment to the group.

On the flip side, there is a correlation between negative leadership behaviours and teams. Team members who experience subversive leaders are less likely to trust their leaders; they have lower job satisfaction and are less likely to remain with the organization.[165] This applies to all levels of leaders. Not surprisingly, one research article[166] identified that when supervisors are abusive to their direct reports, it negatively affects their employees' work behaviour and performance, results in decreased job satisfaction, and, again, lowers the employees' commitment to the organization.

Finally, if we recall from Chapter One, organizations need to develop resiliency and adaptability to be successful. Research has shown that resiliency can be learned and that there is a strong relationship between emotional intelligence and resiliency. Emotional intelligence helps people deal with stressful situations more calmly and therefore make more effective decisions,[167] which is what we need when being resilient.

Learning about and caring for our employees is essential if we move out of an output focus and create long-term sustained growth. It requires leadership courage to open up and be vulnerable. It may feel risky when we share what we're learning and mistakes we've made, but it is through this courage that we create an environment that is safe psychologically and emotionally for our team members – a place where our team members feel cared for.

Leaders as coaches

"The best executive is the one who has sense enough to pick good [people] to do what [they] want to be done, and self-restraint enough to keep from meddling with them while they do it."

- Theodore Roosevelt

The third area for leaders to focus on with their team is their role as a coach. It is through coaching that we increase the capability of our team members. This allows us to more easily delegate knowing that our employees have the skills to do what we ask of them. When we delegate, we get work done through others and we can step out of operational tasks and manage the work of others. Our time is freed up to focus on more strategic work. When we fail to coach, we rob our team members of the opportunity to learn and grow and we rob ourselves of valuable time.

Coaching skills

I'm not suggesting leaders become coaches; rather, leaders need to be more coach-like. There are two aspects of being coach-like. The one we're probably the most familiar with is learning coaching skills – how to ask questions instead of giving advice, using active listening and empathy to connect with the person we're talking with. Often, leaders take a coaching course to learn these skills. While these skills are important, this reflects the left side of the bridge – a formal training course that often has limited applicability and insufficient time to practise the new skills and behaviours.

In his book, *The Coaching Habit: Say Less, Ask More & Change the Way You Lead Forever*,[168] Michael Bungay Stanier provides some concrete practices managers can do to be more coach-like. These are the three I value the most:

- *"Be lazy"* – Don't work so hard. Avoid jumping in to fix things, solve problems, or give answers.
- "Be curious" – Instead of quickly offering advice, be curious and ask questions for a while longer.
- "Be often" – Don't save coaching for performance reviews. Consider each employee interaction as an opportunity for a coaching conversation.

Yes, take courses to learn coaching and develop concrete skills to put into action, but don't stop there. Or rather, don't start there.

Coach identity

The second and more important part of becoming more coach-like is developing a coaching identity. Earlier, I introduced the concept of a 'hero identity' that leaders often adopt if they hold onto operational tasks. It can feel great for a leader to reflect on a day and identify all the fires they've put out. She can feel important and like a hero because so many people came to her, and she had the answers. She feels needed and perhaps indispensable. There's an element of job security. And yet, by controlling information and placing oneself in the centre of the solution, the leader robs their team of developing the skills and experience to solve problems. They remove the employee's opportunity to increase their overall capability. Team members don't learn to identify solutions, think of creative alternatives, or work through the implications of a decision to evaluate its merit. The leader is central to solving problems, but they are also a bottleneck. They stifle their employee's growth and create a dependency that limits both of their ability to develop.

Leaders need to allow others to experiment, find solutions, have missteps, and learn from failures. When their employees succeed, leaders need to step back and let them bask in the spotlight. In doing so, their employees will develop new skills and increase their capability. Over time, the leader's team will increase their capability, allowing them to take on more and allowing the leader more time to focus on strategic initiatives instead of operational tasks. By moving away from a 'hero identity,' the leader also develops new capabilities and can advance their career.

Earlier in this chapter, I introduced a Change Formula to provide a framework for leaders to commit to shifting from an output to a growth-focused workplace. The formula is relevant here, too, as adopting a coach identity can often change leaders' views of themselves. Leaders need to be uncomfortable with the status quo – how they interact with their people, how they are leading or their team's performance. They need to have a vision for how they can lead differently. Once they have discomfort and a vision, leaders can take the first steps, like completing a training course to develop their coaching ability.

You've met Christy Billan a few times already. I want to continue her story to share how she communicated and worked with her team as she transitioned from being a controlling leader to being an empowering one.

Because Christy had been a team member before she started leading her team, she was quite transparent about how she was working on her leadership. She told them she wanted to change her leadership approach, which included empowering them to make decisions, negotiate timelines, and have difficult conversations with each other.

She was clear that she was going to push and coach them as part of this process. Christy also asked her team for help. She said, "If you feel like I'm getting too far into the weeds, and you'd like me to stop, stop me and tell me to coach you." She was explicit about how she wanted her team to raise problems with her. She asked her team to identify if they were sharing the problem as an FYI, to brainstorm solutions, or to escalate and figure out next steps. She found brainstorming could be a 'slippery slope' and lead to solving the problem, so she was conscious and explicit that her role in the brainstorming process was primarily to ask questions.

In our conversation, Christy also shared that leaders need to demonstrate their commitment to learning, by acknowledging and accepting that an employee may be slower in delivering something because it takes time to learn a new skill. Leaders need to create space and set the tone for people to feel comfortable trying new and different things, emphasizing that learning by doing includes being okay to fail. In this way, both the leader and employees need to adjust during this transition.

Christy is long past this transition and has now been operating with a guide-and-empower style of leadership for years. I asked her to reflect on the benefits of the transition. With a laugh, she replied, "My sanity!" She consistently has the capacity to take on more strategic work, which has opened up new career opportunities. She's taken on and expanded into new roles with a broader scope, and she continues to manage it all because her team consistently develops the skills they need to be successful.

She also shared that she is building a 'muscle for the organization.' When the time comes for her to move into a new role, there will be someone who can step into her role. She knows she's not irreplaceable, and ironically, this makes her a better leader.

To shift her leadership and change her identity, Christy needed to solicit the help of her team. There is courage and vulnerability in her approach, which served Christy well as she gained more respect, support, and trust from her team.

Listen to my conversation with Christy in my *Growth through Learning* podcast. Go to **www.hannahbrown.co/resources/podcast** or wherever you find your podcasts.

CHAPTER 11

Organization Support

W e don't work in a vacuum. We work in organizations with cultures, standards, policies, and procedures. The organization in which we work impacts our ability to nurture our Learning Mindset, foster it in others, and create a Team Culture of learning.

If you are a leader in Human Resources or Learning and Development, you might find Learning Mindset and Team Culture resonate from a personal leadership perspective. The third area of focus to achieve a Growth through Learning orientation is Organization Support. If you are an executive with direct influence over your organization's policies, this chapter will provide you with ideas for improving the support you provide to your leaders. If you lead a team of people in a functional area other than Human Resources or Learning and Development, you might want to skim this chapter or skip ahead to the next section – A Focus on Growth.

Our efforts to develop a Growth through Learning orientation can be helped or hindered by our organizations. When leaders complete my diagnostic, Organization Support consistently scores the lowest, after Learning Mindset and Team Culture. Admittedly, it could be that it's always easier to point a finger than look in a mirror. It's easier to find fault with someone or something else, like your organization, than it is to take a look at how your actions contribute to the situation. However, the results of my diagnostic consistently show leaders don't feel supported as they work to embed learning into their teams and coach and develop their employees. There might be an expectation to coach and support direct reports, but it isn't supported with opportunities to develop leadership skills. There might be a disconnect between the organization encouraging coaching, yet not prioritizing access to learning tools and support. As one leader shared in my diagnostic, "I never really felt like I was supposed to use my professional development budget, it always seemed like a perk that looks good on paper."

There are three areas where organizations need to support their leaders in developing a Growth through Learning orientation: clear expectations, access to resources, and celebration of their efforts. Let's look at these to understand what organizations can do to better support their leaders.

Clear expectations

"All of us perform better and more willingly when we know why we're doing what we have been told or asked to do."

– Kenneth Blanchard

Organization Support begins with setting clear expectations for leaders. In Chapter Six, we looked at how the Growth Equation identifies where leaders can have the greatest impact on their employees' growth. Leaders need to start with direction and feedback, provide tools and resources, and then create an environment conducive to learning and growth. So, too, organizations need to start with direction and feedback and set clear expectations. Leaders need to know if coaching and developing employees for growth is part of their mandate as leaders.

> *Mary[xi] is the director of Corporate Brand and Social Responsibility at a national charitable organization. She currently leads a small team but over the years has led teams of up to 60 employees. We talked about the relationship between leaders who coach and develop their employees, and the support they receive from their organization to help them be successful.*
>
> *Mary's organization is explicitly clear that a leader's role is to invest in and develop their employees. They need*

(xi) Name has been changed to maintain anonymity.

to work with their employees to build long-term plans for growth and learning. The organization has an internal brand with 10 leadership commitments that are formalized and describe what all leaders are expected to do, including developing their people. The leadership commitments firmly anchor and define the culture within the organization. Employees are aware of the commitments, so there's two-way accountability. The leader is accountable to themselves and the organization, and the employee can hold the leader accountable.

Mary also differentiated her role as a leader from that of Human Resources. They have subject matter experts who can help shape the development plans for her employees, but she needs to identify the challenge or opportunity. It's not HR's job to identify performance or growth. Once she's identified that as the leader, HR can suggest options to address it.

Mary provides a helpful example of how organizations can be explicit about their expectations of leaders. She also emphasizes how leaders and support functions, like Human Resources, work together to coach and develop employees.

A first step organizations can take is incorporating employee learning into the leader's objectives in their performance management system. In a McKinsey and Company podcast, Matthew Smith, Partner and former Chief Learning Officer in McKinsey's Paris office, talks about the benefit of leaders in creating learning and development plans with their employees and having ongoing conversations with them about how they are doing against that plan. It's more than tracking hours spent in courses and provides a more effective way of embedding learning and development into the organization's culture.[169]

The leader's role is to nurture a Learning Mindset and develop a Team Culture focused on learning. These efforts need to rest on a foundation of growth through learning across the organization. Otherwise, the leader will be swimming against the current. They will be trying to coach and grow their employees, but in an environment that doesn't support, value, or reward that behaviour.

In addition to being explicit about the leaders' role in coaching for personal growth, organizations need to be congruent. What's outlined in a policy, job description, or performance management system needs to align with the broader organization's culture. While leaders say they value learning, employees often have no more than 1% of their time available for learning.[170] Learning takes time and can be messy. When people try new things, they make mistakes. If an organization punishes people for making mistakes, employees will shy away from learning.[171] When an organization's expectations are clearly stated but negated because the workplace culture overrides it, it's worse than having no expectations at all.

When organizations provide clear expectations of their leaders and prioritize employee learning and development alongside getting results, leaders can align their identity and practices to the broader expectations. They are supported and feel like their values align with the organization. Instead of feeling like their professional development budget is a perk on paper, they feel like it's a resource they can actually use.

Connected to resources

"Information is a source of learning.
But unless it is organized, processed, and available
to the right people in a format for decision making,
it is a burden, not a benefit."

– C. William Pollard

In addition to having clearly defined and aligned expectations, organizations need to provide resources to their leaders. Larger organizations typically offer more robust internal training programs and external opportunities for professional development (e.g., conferences, professional certifications, or degrees). Referring back to the Growth Equation, this is the organizational equivalent of tools and resources. In smaller organizations, this may be limited to a professional development policy and an employee professional development allowance.

> *Chantal McIntyre is a talent strategist, workplace*
> *consultant, and leadership coach with her own consulting*
> *practice. She partners with CEOs and leaders to create*
> *customized talent strategies, which has provided her with*
> *a rich perspective on the critical role that leaders play*
> *in coaching and developing their teams. Chantal shared*
> *the unique challenges facing leaders in small to medium-*
> *sized organizations.*
>
> *In companies with around 250 employees, it is common*
> *to have a Human Resources specialist, but often there isn't*

a dedicated learning and development professional. In this gap, leaders turn to Human Resource professionals, who may or may not have the necessary background in learning and development to effectively support their teams.

While many organizations default to formal training programs, doing so is not the only or the best way to develop employees. Adopting a Growth through Learning orientation helps small and medium-sized organizations do more with less. It embeds learning in the organization's DNA, so there's less reliance on expensive, formal training programs.

Listen to my conversation with Chantal in my *Growth through Learning* podcast. Go to **www.hannahbrown.co/resources/podcast** or wherever you find your podcasts.

Returning to my bridge analogy from the Preface, this is where both sides of the bridge come together. Well-designed and well-implemented formal training programs allow employees to learn new skills. Onboarding programs quickly orient new employees to the organization, their team, and their role. Training to meet compliance and regulatory requirements is another opportunity for formal training to shine. Well-designed e-learning can be a cost-effective way to ensure employees are aware of privacy and security procedures, anti-harassment policies, etc. Management development programs help new supervisors and leaders learn foundational skills in the 'mechanics' of leading others – the organization's people policies, performance management, hiring process, etc. These programs can also introduce them to the people side of leading – communication skills, giving feedback, and such.

For these programs to be effective and span across the bridge, they need to be targeted to the audience, well-designed to avoid content dumps, and implemented to accommodate the audience's circumstances. Too often, participants say training time is wasted because it's not relevant, of poor quality, and not aligned to what they actually need.

Let me expand on onboarding programs as one example where formal training has an important role in employee development. Importantly, onboarding validates the employee's decision to join. Onboarding must go beyond compliance and role expectations and orient new employees to the organization's and team's values and culture. It must help the new employee connect with colleagues and access relevant information and resources.

I've been working with a division in a regional municipality to improve their onboarding experience for new employees. Human Resources provides new employee orientation focused on personal administration, policies, mandatory training, etc. My client, Richard, wanted a more robust onboarding program that reflected the technical aspects and the culture of his division. He wanted new employees to feel connected to their leaders, peers, and teams even when working remotely. His division leadership acknowledged that the coming years would see an increasing percentage of senior people close to retirement, and he wanted to tap into their expertise and transfer their institutional knowledge to new employees before they

retired. Further, staff turnover had been consistently high
for many years, compromising the team's bench strength.
The onboarding programs we created incorporated
existing content, provided new material, and, most impor-
tantly, focused on connecting the new employee with their
supervisor, a peer mentor, and colleagues in their division.

The case for a strong onboarding program is compelling. Gallup[172] estimates that only 12% of employees agree that their organization does a great job onboarding new employees. Nearly one-third of all new hires quit their job within the first six months,[173] which suggests their initial experience with their new organization wasn't positive. It costs companies six to nine months of an employee's salary to recruit, hire and onboard a replacement.[174] So, for an employee who earns $80,000, it costs between $40,000 and $60,000 to hire a replacement!

Leaders and organizations also need to look beyond onboarding to ensure employees learn and grow throughout their tenure. They need to look beyond formal training to ensure employees are learning and developing throughout their career.

"If they're not growing, they're going."

– Hannah Brown

This has been the experience of another client I work with. They wanted a more intentional approach to employee professional development and to providing a career path for employees. Among their most pressing concerns was the need to address their turnover. In analyzing their employee data from a development lens, it became clear that the greatest desire for learning and growth came from these two groups:

- Employees in junior positions in their first year of working. They're new and eager to learn all that they can.
- Employees in leadership roles who don't manage a team. They're ready for the next step and are looking for ways to develop skills to lead others.

The data also revealed that these two groups represented their greatest 'flight risk.' Employees in these groups are hungry to learn, and if they don't grow, they leave. The DDI Global Leadership Forecast study identified that employees are 2.2 times more likely to leave their current role if they are under the age of 35.[175]

I worked with this client to introduce a career pathing program that identified ways for employees to develop. The program outlined roles and expectations for employees, leaders and Human Resources.

Through this program, my client clarified the expectations of leaders to guide employee development. They provided resources and support to both leaders and team members. Employees developed in their current role and prepared for a new role – whether a promotion or a lateral move. Yes, there's a risk that leaders invest time and effort into an employee who leaves. There's an equally high possibility that the employee will feel cared for and stay with the organization because of the manager's relationship and because they are learning new skills.

Organizations with established training departments often overlook the importance of non-formal training resources. Checklists and how-to guides are great examples of informal resources that support leaders in developing employees and creating a culture of learning at a team level. Creating these resources can be in the domain of the training department. Better yet, leaders and their teams can take ownership of documenting their processes and best practices. The role of the training department then is to function as a business partner, as described in Chapter Two. This means they understand their business units and bring a learning lens to procedure documents and reference guides so they are targeted and easy to use.

I worked for a medium-sized government agency, and my team created user-friendly reference guides and how-to job aids for a complex data capture and analysis system. They had dense 40-page reference manuals that thoroughly documented all possible tasks and uses. The challenge was that the manuals were so comprehensive that users found it difficult to find the specific piece of information they needed. My team divided the content into role-specific and task-specific job aids that users could access depending on their role and what task they needed help with.

This is an example of how a learning and development department can extend its reach from the left side of the bridge to meet leaders and their teams in the middle.

The important thing with resources is that employees and leaders know they exist and are able to access them. I've been working with a government organization for several years to help them embed learning and development into established processes to help existing employees continue to grow and learn. Like many government organizations, they have a plethora of resources available, but staff don't know about them or can't find them. There are huge inefficiencies as employees look for what they need, save a local copy and then don't receive updates. They work from outdated materials. Training is often a one-time event for existing staff and training materials are created for system launches and upgrades. Materials are archived, but there isn't a sustainment plan for new employees so the benefits of the initial training and materials are lost. When supervisors and managers want to reinforce the training or develop new employees, finding these resources can be like looking for a needle in a haystack. By one estimate, employees spend on average 20% of their workweek looking for internal information or finding colleagues who can help with specific tasks.[176] Think of the wasted time and lost productivity!

Resources can be policies, training courses, or physical artifacts like the job aids my team created. Resources can also be processes and frameworks leaders can use, especially when they are new to leadership.

> *Matthew[(xii)] is a manager in the Project Management Office at a medium-sized technology company. After a long career drawing on his engineering and technical skills, he moved from managing a project team to managing a team of direct reports. When Matthew and I talked, he shared some of his initial experiences leading people. He talked about his organization's performance management process and the structure it provided in his early days of*

(xii)   Name has been changed to maintain anonymity.

leading others. His role was to help his employees identify their goals and ensure they aligned with broader team goals and the organization's overall goals. Goals supported employees' regular tasks and focused on developing skills in their current and possible future roles. Initially, Matthew's performance conversations focused on goals and tasks. He's transitioned from these more project management-type conversations to having regular check-in meetings where employees take the lead and provide an update on what they're working on, what they're struggling with, and where they need support. These reflect a broader performance and development focus.

Matthew's experience highlights the need for organizations to create frameworks or systems to support leaders as they start to coach and develop their people. A leader can initiate these conversations within a performance management process and, over time and with more experience, incorporate additional conversations focused on specific developmental goals.

When leaders aren't supported by their organization, they struggle to lead effectively, or are unable to lead at all.

Maria[(xiii)] is a manager at a Canadian financial institution. When we talked about her journey as a leader, she shared a beautiful contrast between the leader she tried to be and failed at miserably, and the successful leader she is today. Maria describes her early unsuccessful leadership experience as an "epic fail." She was offered the job and

---

(xiii) Name has been changed to maintain anonymity.

turned it down three times before she finally accepted it. She felt she was too inexperienced but was told, "You'll be fine. You have good instincts. It's a small district that you're managing." When she started, she realized she didn't know how to lead the team. Her instincts weren't enough, and the district was larger than she could manage. In addition, she didn't receive the support she needed. She was geographically isolated and didn't have guidance from a mentor or senior leaders. After a short time in the position, she was moved into a different role. Maria said it took her eight years to recover from that experience.

Now Maria is in a management role in a different area and is more effective and much happier. She has experience under her belt and used her 'epic fail' as an opportunity to reflect and learn. She's also leaning into the support her organization provides. She has a mentor, peers, and leadership support. Her director and VP both support and guide her. Her philosophy now as a leader is to learn from your mistakes. She borrows a saying from her director, "Let's forget the mistake, learn the lesson. If you don't learn the lesson, then that's a performance issue, but let's... let's forget the mistake and learn first."

Resources are one way to connect the left and right sides of the bridge. They extend from the Human Resource or Learning and Development department to leaders so they can create a culture of learning on their teams and adopt a Growth through Learning orientation. Leaders and their teams don't work in isolation. Their efforts are impacted by the organization in which they work. When organizations provide resources that are easy to access, leaders' efforts are leveraged and more effective.

Celebrated successes

"It's always good to remember where you come from and celebrate it. To remember where you come from is part of where you're going."

– Anthony Burgess

Once leaders are clear about the organization's expectations of them and have the resources to be successful, their efforts need to be celebrated. This is the organizational equivalent of environment in the Growth Equation. Celebration includes recognition and reward.

Recognition

Research shows there's a strong correlation between recognition and cost savings. For example, Gallup calculated that when employee recognition is part of an organization's culture, a 10,000-employee organization can save up to $16.1 million annually due to reduced turnover.[177] They found that one in four employees strongly agreed that they had received recognition for doing good work in the previous week. In their analysis, they calculated that if companies could double this number – increase it from one in four to two in four – they would experience a 9% improvement in productivity and a 22% decrease in absenteeism. Both of these measures contribute to an organization's overall profitability, growth, and success.

Recognition increases productivity because it impacts employee motivation. As explored in Chapter Six with the Growth Equation, motivation can be extrinsic or intrinsic. We often think of extrinsic motivation first – salary, compensation, etc. – but it is intrinsic motivation that is more powerful and sustains employee work over the long term. Recognition directly taps into motivation by celebrating individual work, bonding a team, and connecting personal achievement to organizational success.[178]

Recognition also decreases employee absenteeism because of the connection to intrinsic motivation. When people receive recognition, they take pride in what they do. They are more likely to show up and keep showing up even when things are difficult. Recognition may also decrease employee absenteeism because of its impact on mental health. Recognition acts as a buffer against job stress.[179] It positively impacts employees and gives them the energy and resiliency to show up and keep persevering.

If you have ownership for recognition in your organization, you may be thinking, "Great, how do I incorporate more recognition into our organization?" It doesn't have to be complicated. My teenage son works as a lifeguard and swim instructor. His pool has a practice of recognizing staff. They give out stars for work well done and when staff go above and beyond what's expected. The stars are posted in the guard office for everyone to see. At the end of each month, a name is drawn randomly and the employee receives a gift certificate for a coffee shop.

If you want something more robust, here are five considerations[180] to keep in mind.

- Fulfilling – Ensure the recognition is proportionate and appropriate to the accomplishment.
- Authentic – Be genuine in your recognition; be less formal.
- Personalized – Tailor the recognition to the individual; consider if they prefer public or more private praise.
- Equitable – Ensure you focus on achievement and not favouritism.
- Embedded – Once you start, embed recognition into your team's values and practices.

Where is the opportunity to recognize your leaders' efforts in coaching and developing their employees?

Reward

Celebrating leaders' success also includes rewards. This relates to external motivators and is about leaders' compensation. One common model is pay for performance, which ties compensation directly to performance through a bonus or commission. It's common with salespeople who usually have clearly defined sales targets. Compensating leaders for employee learning and growth requires specific Key Performance Indicators, which can be difficult to define with equity and implement with transparency.

Another common approach is skill-based compensation, which encourages ongoing learning and development. Employees are incentivized to acquire new skills that can lead to higher pay. As an example, a growing technology company may adopt this approach and increase the salaries of employees who obtain certificates in new technologies. While this may be appropriate for a fast-growing company in a quickly changing industry like information technology, it would be less appropriate for a stable organization like a financial institution or government agency.

Regardless of the overall approach and the specific nuances of the program, it's critical that leaders are rewarded for their efforts to coach and develop employees.

Developing a Growth through Learning orientation requires focusing on three areas:

- Learning Mindset
- Team Culture
- Organization Support.

Leaders need to nurture their own Learning Mindset through curiosity by being courageous and consistent and developing a habit of lifelong learning. Leaders must also foster this in their teams by developing a Team Culture of learning. This starts with leaders committing to coach and develop employees. To act on this commitment, leaders need to care about their employees in a personal way. This means opening up themselves and relating to them as people, not just employees. Caring for employees requires emotional intelligence – the ability to manage our emotions and understand the emotions of others. In doing so, leaders create a team environment where taking risks and experimenting is okay and failure is viewed as an opportunity to learn, not a reason to be fired. For leaders to create a Team Culture of learning, they need to adopt a coach-like mindset and identity. They ask questions more and provide advice less often. This creates space for team members to learn and develop new skills.

Finally, leaders work and lead within their organization's structure and culture. To be successful, organizations need to provide leaders with clear expectations that align with their culture and practices. Organizations also need to provide resources so leaders can confidently coach and develop employees, and celebrate leaders' achievements through recognition and compensation.

These areas of focus – Learning Mindset, Team Culture, and Organization Support – foster a Growth through Learning orientation. This propels organizations out of an output-focused workplace and prepares them for long-term sustained growth. As leaders like Christy Billan build muscles and the capabilities of their team, organizations can focus on growth for their future.

A Focus on Growth

"As we look ahead into the next century, leaders will be those who empower others."

– Bill Gates

CHAPTER 12

A Growth-Focused Workplace

N o matter your industry or the size of your organization, you can prioritize learning alongside results and develop a Growth through Learning orientation. This sets the stage for building a long-term sustained future for you, your employees, and your organization.

Lina Shamoun is the owner and principal stylist at Artline Salon in Kitchener, Ontario. She is a phenomenal stylist and, for years, has competed in hair competitions around the world (I had no idea there was such a thing when I first met her!). We talked about my book the last time she cut my hair.

Lina's salon has about eight staff. It isn't possible to send a stylist to a course to further their career or develop new skills. Yet, Lina believes in the importance of ongoing learning and development.

She wanted her stylists to be more creative, take more risks, and be more artistic. Instead of an expensive course, Lina signed them up for a competition. They had an intensive three – to six – month preparation period and then travelled to the nationals to compete. They were motivated because they had a common goal and a specific deadline. Lina said that what they learned in that period of time was more than they would have learned in two years of cutting hair. And, when they went to the competition, they won! Their awards now decorate the walls in the salon.

Lina also entered the competition, so she role-modelled the preparation and process before and during the event. They learned and travelled together, which brought them closer as a team.

Lina shared that often in her industry, stylists are discredited because, historically, it wasn't considered a profession. Stylists were high-school dropouts, and the job was something people (often women) turned to after having children. Being a hair stylist was a fall-back job, not an intentional career.

Lina is an exceptionally capable stylist and equally successful businesswoman. By providing her team with the learning experience of a competition, she elevated their capabilities as stylists, bonded them as a team and created a differentiator for her salon for her customers. "We are award-winning!" Lina is changing what it means to be a stylist and is doing it through a focus on learning and growth. A formal course wasn't the answer – it's too expensive and wouldn't have resulted in the rich learning the competition provided.

Lina's story provides an example of the importance learning and growth has on an individual, a team, and a business. It also gives us a beautiful example of how, even in a small business, a leader can prioritize growth through learning. You met Christine Helgerman, Director of St. John's Christian Nursery School, in Chapter Three. While a bit larger than Lina's salon, her school provides another example of how learning and growth can be embedded into the culture of a smaller organization.

Christine describes herself as a fast mover and likes it when people match her speed. However, she's learned that her pace and approach are less effective than a more collaborative approach. Now she takes more time, knowing her team will get there and be more motivated and committed to the decision. While she may get results sooner with her faster natural pace, the benefits of a slower inclusive approach outweigh her solo approach to decision-making and leading.

Christine sets the goal for her team and then together they determine the best approach to take. The goal can be based on a vision or an established policy. The approach might be something new the team agrees upon or simply refining a procedure.

Christine's team members contribute to discussions and provide their perspectives. Even if they don't agree with the final decision, they support the decision knowing they were heard and will be able to share their opinions in future discussions. As a leader, Christine benefits from the collective approach because of the shared responsibility for the outcome. If a mistake is made or something goes wrong, it doesn't all rest on her shoulders. The team collectively owns it, discusses it, and learns how to do it differently next time. The board of directors also benefits because they have greater confidence in the staff's ability to implement decisions successfully.

Given St. John's size and fixed budget, I was curious how Christine incorporates employee development into her leadership. Capacity building is at the core of what she does. She works to people's strengths and finds opportunities for them to take on special projects based on their interests, such as creating social media, submitting applications to governing bodies, or spearheading a community event. Her role is to support her team by providing resources, time, and guidance.

Christine's leadership provides a beautiful example of the impact one person – the leader – can have on an organization. The average tenure for early learning educators in a nursery school is 5 to 7 years. Christine's staff have been with St. John's for an average of 12 to 15 years, and there are three who have tenures of 23 years! When I take my kids back to visit, which I've done many times over the years, I know that while there will be some new faces, there will also be some staff who have remained.

Christine's leadership also provides an example of how a high-functioning team that continues to grow through learning impacts its customers. Christine perhaps knows this instinctually, but the research[181] shows that a team culture of learning supports customer satisfaction. Employees are more engaged with customers and listen to their opinions, both positive and negative. When they feel supported and psychologically safe, employees feel free to question the customer journey and suggest process improvements. Christine's staff are included in decision making and are empowered to make changes to meet the needs of their children and families.

I was a St. John's customer over a decade ago. I've returned with my kids for visits several times over the years. Think of your past customers or employees – who has kept in touch, and what does that suggest about your organization and leadership?

Listen to my conversation with Christine in my *Growth through Learning* podcast. Go to **www.hannahbrown.co/resources/podcast** or wherever you find your podcasts.

Let me circle back to a research article I introduced in Chapter One. McKinsey analyzed about 2,000 organizations and identified that those with a dual focus on performance and people have a competitive advantage over their peers. McKinsey called these organizations P+P Winners. These organizations have a collaborative, challenging, yet nurturing environment. I identify these organizations as having a Growth through Learning orientation. By focusing on learning, they have moved away from a short-term focus on output and into a longer-term sustained focus on growth. Let's look at leaders' behaviours and their employees' experiences in a growth-focused workplace.

CHAPTER 13
How Leaders Create a Growth-Focus

"If I am hit by a bus, would St. John's continue
without me? Twenty years ago, maybe not,
but now, absolutely. A good leader can walk away,
and the organization can keep going.
If a leader walks away and it falls apart,
maybe the leader hasn't done their part."

– Christine Helgerman

When leaders embrace a Growth through Learning orientation, they are focused on building a team and a legacy for the future. A leader who is building a future is a learner first. They continue to be curious about new perspectives and are open to experimenting with new ways for their team to work.

In Chapter Eleven you met Mary, the director of Corporate Brand and Social Responsibility at a national charitable organization. She shared how her organization has explicit expectations and 10 leadership commitments that guide how to be a leader. Mary also shared how her personal learning and encouragement of learning in her team go hand in hand.

"I know I'm evolving every day as a leader. I think there are two buckets I need to focus on. There's my professional designation and how I need to keep on top of industry trends and grow and learn. There's a whole world evolving around us that we need to stay on top of. I also think leadership is a journey and that's separate from my professional expertise. That's about everyday coaching conversations. Every moment is an opportunity to learn. So I think those two buckets are really important. I think it's great to be vulnerable with employees and share your own leadership journey to say, 'This is where I am struggling' or, 'This is what I'm learning' or, 'This is what I've just learned, and maybe it could help you.'"

Mary and I also talked about her personal leadership philosophy, which is anchored in caring about her employees as human beings. She's focused on building relationships and long-term development plans, which means that she needs to know her employees' goals and objectives and understand them as people. She needs to make sure the direction they want to go aligns with the organization.

I asked Mary what it looks like when things don't work well between leaders and their employees. What are the aspects that fall apart? "First and foremost, [things fall apart] when employees feel that a leader doesn't care about them as a professional or as a human." All leaders are under pressure to deliver, and so the organization needs to have success and accountability measures to make sure that leaders are taking the time for learning and development. Leaders need to protect the time to have regular meetings with employees about their professional development and career goals, not just once at performance review time. The focus really is on long-term career planning. Mary summarized it nicely by saying, "Bottom line, my role is to help people who work for me advance and grow up and take on more responsibility and become leaders. And I think that's my end goal – if you're in the same role five years later, with no room for growth or development, I haven't done my job."

Mary's story provides a great example of embracing a long-term perspective and focus on employee development. This is coupled with her earlier story of how her organization has explicit expectations of leaders to coach and develop their employees.

Leaders focused on growth accept the risks of their curiosity, knowing it may lead them to try new approaches that could fail. Calculated experiments form the foundation of learning. In Chapter One, you met Larry, who works in a medium-sized technology organization; Larry's team member, Barbara, gained new skills that she applied more strategically across the organization. Larry also shared how he encourages his team to experiment.

> *Larry works for a fast-paced technology company where creativity and innovation are part of the company culture. Larry explained that the culture he's nurtured in his team is one of collaboration, trust and experimentation. Employees come to Larry with ideas for new processes or approaches to problems. As the leader, his responsibility is to help the employee define a clear goal. Larry is very data-driven, so he also identifies the metrics of success. He doesn't prescribe the solution because this is his employee's idea; they are the expert. Larry is the guide who provides company context and support. He also assesses the risk of the idea or experiment to determine the possibility and severity of it completely failing. If the stakes are too high, they figure out if they can mitigate the risks enough to continue. Larry works with the employee as the experiment unfolds to continue guiding and providing resources as needed.*
>
> *Larry explained that his team's culture of experimentation recognizes that things usually don't go perfectly the first time or even subsequent times. Experimenting is an iterative process where, after each setback, they evaluate what happened, learn from it, and try again with a slightly different approach based on what they learned.*
>
> *Ultimately, Larry's role is to take the heat if the experiment fails and let his employees receive the accolades if successful.*

I love Larry's approach to experimentation and the iterative nature that assumes failures will occur. Failures offer insights and data points to learn from, and that can be used to inform the next experiment. In her book, *Right Kind of Wrong: The Science of Failing Well*,[182] Amy Edmondson discusses different types of mistakes:

- Basic failures that should be minimized.
- Complex failures that need to be anticipated and mitigated.
- Intelligent failures to promote and celebrate because they inform our learning.

These types of mistakes align with Larry's approach where he helps define the goal and assess the risks. As leaders, we want to encourage experimentation and risk-taking in our teams and focus on intelligent failures.

Making mistakes and building a culture of trust was also a theme in my conversation with Len Switzer. Len is currently an adjunct instructor in chemical engineering at Michigan Technical University. He's also had a long and successful career in industry, having had various leadership roles in manufacturing, oil, and gas.

Several times, Len has stepped in to lead a team that's struggling, with the intention of turning it around. The team is in survival mode – not functioning well. They don't trust each other and don't communicate with each other. They don't share mistakes for fear of reprimand, including being fired.

Len shared that when he leads these teams, his first priority is to establish trust. Without trust, nothing else will work. He's been asked what his secret sauce is. "It's not a secret. It's pretty basic really – it's listening and empathy."

Basic perhaps, but not easy to do! Len talked about getting to know his team individually both professionally and person- ally. "Having a beer together? That's the important event."

Len is an engineer, and so has an extensive education which prioritizes passing tests and proving that he knows everything. That need for indisputable knowledge continues into the workplace, where engineers are seen as the experts. Len explained that it can take a long time for people to come off their pedestals and realize that the collective mind is far more powerful than the individual mind.

Len has embraced this and role models asking ques- tions and listening before giving advice and answers. When people come to him and are unsure about how to do something, he takes the time to coach and teach them. They focus on the big picture and he ensures the employee has ownership of the details.

The metaphor Len has is that of a parent teaching a child to ride a bike – holding the seat until they can balance on their own and then letting go.

Listen to my conversation with Len in my *Growth through Learning* podcast. Go to **www.hannahbrown.co/resources/podcast** or wherever you find your podcasts.

Larry and Len's experiences speak to the importance of trust, open communication, and the role experimentation has in find- ing creative solutions and ongoing innovation. This is relevant to medium-sized organizations like the ones Len worked for, and smaller organizations like where Larry works. Often, small and medium enterprises have unique challenges. Let's revisit Chantal McIntyre, whom you met in Chapter Eleven and who works with this size of organization, to hear her perspective.

> Chantal has observed that some leaders may get stuck in a fixed mindset, often due to the demands and pressures of their roles, and unintentionally deprioritize their own learning. This can create challenges in fostering a culture of learning within their teams, as the focus often shifts to immediate results and meeting short-term goals. These leaders may be driven by external factors such as performance metrics or bonuses, which can limit both their own potential and their team's long-term success.
>
> In contrast, Chantal highlights leaders who embrace lifelong learning and are deeply committed to developing their people. "These leaders are less focused on 'me' and more on 'we.' They're dedicated to being the kind of leader people want to follow, rather than just the kind of leader who gets results at any cost for higher compensation." By prioritizing relationships and people development, these leaders create stronger, more sustainable outcomes.

Chantal's experience underscores the powerful connection between a leader's motivation and identity and their ability to foster growth in others.

Listen to my conversation with Chantal in my *Growth through Learning* podcast. Go to **www.hannahbrown.co/resources/podcast** or wherever you find your podcasts.

Andrew Ambrose is another leader who recognizes that growth and learning go hand in hand. Andrew is the director of Learning at Aecon Group Inc., a North American construction and infrastructure development company headquartered in Toronto. Andrew leads a team of learning and development professionals who design and deliver a range of courses to their leaders, employees, and contractors.

As a fellow leader in learning and development, Andrew shares a bias for learning and developing others. In leading his team, he recognizes they need to balance doing repetitive work that's perhaps a bit boring, with more creative work where they can bring their passion. Andrew's team attended the Canadian National Learning and Development Conference last year. However, in our conversation, he focused on the informal learning opportunities and the day-to-day experiences he provides to keep his team engaged, learning, and passionate. Andrew leverages his experienced staff to support folks who are newer in their careers. He asks his team to share work they've done in other companies to 'feed the beast' and add creative ideas to their work.

Andrew and I also talked about the importance of team dynamics and culture. "What a difference it makes when a team is really gelled. They're not going through intermediaries; they're solving problems together. They're collaborating to find solutions."

Andrew described this as the "holy grail." If you can get to this point where the team is comfortable with each other and supports each other, it's a good indicator that things are going well and the team is healthy. When leaders aren't interested in developing people and are just trying to get things out the door, they're focused on short-term results. "What you end up getting is short-term employment as well."

Employees are unhappy and there's higher turnover. Andrew acknowledged that most leaders have their one or two 'go-tos' – people they know can take on a difficult project or solve a complex problem. Andrew challenges this and says everyone on a team needs to be a 'go-to.'

What a great perspective and personal challenge this is for leaders! Coach and develop your people so they're all 'go-to' people.

Listen to my conversation with Andrew in my *Growth through Learning* podcast. Go to **www.hannahbrown.co/resources/podcast** or wherever you find your podcasts.

The concept of 'a rising tide lifts all boats' comes to mind when I think of having a team full of 'go-to' people. When leaders invest in themselves and their teams, team members develop new skills and increase their capability. Through stronger relationships, leaders and team members develop trust, which creates space for experimenting, taking risks, learning, and growth.

Finally, you met Robin Young, director of Corporate Training Services at Durham College, in Chapter Six where he described a past organization's top-down and bottom-up approach that prioritized results above all else.

> *Robin also described leaders whose success metric is the*
> *quality of their relationships and connections instead of*
> *performance and business results. These leaders know you*
> *can't get measurable business change without people.*

When leaders create an environment of trust, like Robin has, they become talent magnets. Employees want to work for them and will switch teams or leave organizations to follow their leaders.

Listen to my conversation with Robin in my *Growth through Learning* podcast. Go to **www.hannahbrown.co/resources/podcast** or wherever you find your podcasts.

How often have you been on the receiving end of this? You've started a new role leading an existing team, and before your people get to know you, they leave to follow their old manager. Be the leader others want to follow and create the team everyone wants to be a part of.

CHAPTER 14

Employees in a Growth-Focused Workplace

I t's just so much more enjoyable to work on a team with a strong capable leader who has created a sense of camaraderie and connection. You feel your contributions matter and you can see a future for yourself. You won't be stuck in the same role doing the same work five years from now. I'm sure if you reflect on your career, there are teams that stand out as shining examples and others that are dull in comparison.

When we work on teams where our leaders encourage and prioritize learning and growth, we feel energized, committed, and hopeful about our work on the team and in the organization. When leaders create a team culture focused on growth and the future, team members feel cared for, safe, and motivated to do their best work.

You were reintroduced to Robin Young in the previous chapter. Here are some insights into how employees experience him as a leader.

> *Robin creates a team culture where his employees feel cared for – their work, their personal selves and their career. They feel understood, and so can do their best work. There is trust between Robin and his team, who knows he has confidence in them to do great work. They are encouraged to be curious and pursue experiments, knowing if they fail, they will not be reprimanded but will work through their experience with Robin to learn from it.*

When I read about how employees experience working on Robin's team, I recall the importance of creating a psychologically safe space for people to work, learn, and grow. I've known Robin for a decade and worked with him for about half that time. I know Robin is a talent magnet, a leader others want to follow, and that he leads a team others want to join.

Listen to my conversation with Robin in my *Growth through Learning* podcast. Go to **www.hannahbrown.co/resources/podcast** or wherever you find your podcasts.

Employees do better when they work on teams where learning is a focus. Employees who spend time learning on the job are 47% less likely to be stressed and 21% more likely to feel confident.[183] They are more committed to their organization when their managers support their ongoing learning and development, which turns 'quiet quitters' into engaged team members and reduces their intention to leave.[184]

I want to share a more in-depth story to paint a full picture of what a leader does when they focus on growth through learning and, importantly, what their employees experience.

Andy Rombouts is the newly retired director of Support Services for London Health Sciences Centre (LHSC). His portfolio included patient food services, portering, switchboard medical device processing, retail food, contract linen, and the housekeeping contract. There are over 500 people on the team with about 17 leaders. Housekeeping has an additional 500 people led by their leadership team. So, a pretty significant portfolio in a large facility.

When I talked with Andy, he was about to transition into retirement and had a wealth of experience to share. Since his early career days, Andy's leadership philosophy has been centred on creating a culture that recognizes and supports others. His team is a place where people can grow, ask questions, and critique situations in healthy debate. As a result, Andy's portfolio has a tremendously stable leadership team, which can backfill leadership and critical positions seamlessly. The portfolio is structured with a director, managers, and coordinators, all of whom are in leadership roles. They also have advisors, who are individual contributors learning coordinator role skills. Even with the stability of the team, turnover happens. If a coordinator leaves, an advisor can step into the role because they have been learning aspects of the role and have had some exposure to the role. They have a manager and director to support them, so their chance of success is quite high. Andy shared a comment a colleague made to him in 2020 – that it no longer feels like a dead-end job for front-line staff. The succession planning approach provides internal advancement and opportunity for all employees.

Andy, facing his retirement, provided another example of successful succession planning. He talked about the managers reporting to him and his confidence that one of them could step into his role; he knows it would be almost seamless. In contrast, if they hired an external candidate, it would take six months for that person to learn about LHSC and another six to learn about the leadership team and the rest of the employees. During that time, there would be disruption in service, increased workload for others, and stress throughout the transition. So, developing employees for their current role and future roles benefits the employee and the organization.

Finally, Andy shared a third example where a manager in a very technical role with a longstanding career at LHSC was retiring. They hired a coordinator early so they could learn all the details of the role alongside the existing manager. When the manager retired, the coordinator transitioned into the role with minimal disruption. The whole organization was comfortable and confident in the change in leadership and transfer of knowledge.

Andy's experience highlights the importance of a leadership approach that emphasizes employee learning and development. He created a Team Culture of learning that cascaded throughout his 500+ team. The benefits are clear. Employees from front-line positions through to leadership roles could see opportunities for career growth and advancement. Leaders developed teams capable of backfilling critical roles. The organization repeatedly experienced a seamless transition of leadership.

When Andy and I talked, we were about two years past the

COVID-19 pandemic, which saw tremendous upheaval for healthcare centres and workers across the globe. After passing the acute crisis phase, healthcare continued to struggle as burn-out set in. In 2020, 30% to 40% of healthcare workers experienced burnout. In the spring of 2021, that increased to over 60%.[185] In Canada, nurses, in particular, were leaving the profession at about double the rate compared to before the pandemic.[186] The stability of Andy's team during this time is a tremendous testament to his leadership and the culture of learning and growth he created.

Listen to my conversation with Andy in my *Growth through Learning* podcast. Go to **www.hannahbrown.co/resources/podcast** or wherever you find your podcasts.

When leaders embrace a Growth through Learning orientation, nurture their own Learning Mindset, and foster a Team Culture of learning, they build a team and an organization for the future. Microsoft Corporation provides a beautiful example of an organization that shifted its culture from complacency to renewed innovation. Upon becoming the CEO in 2014, Satya Nadella's goal was to change the culture from a place where people acted like 'know-it-alls' to one where they acted like 'learn-it-alls.' He moved the organization toward a Team Culture of learning.[187]

If you lead in a small or medium-sized organization and have been reading this, you may wonder how you can shift from an output focus into a growth focus. Perhaps you feel like you need more budget or formal training programs. Perhaps you're tempted to stretch your budget and hire a learning and development professional. Let me circle back to Lina at Artline Salon, and Christine at St. John's. Both are small organizations without a training or even a Human Resources department. They don't have access to formal training programs. Instead, they focus on nurturing a Learning Mindset and creating a Team Culture of learning. They create opportunities to learn and grow within their organization and through external experiences. It's their leadership and culture that creates long-term sustained growth and positions them for the future.

Conclusion

"Learning is not compulsory; it's voluntary...
But to survive, we must learn."

– W. Edwards Deming

CHAPTER 15
Summary

For organizations to thrive in our volatile, uncertain, complex, and ambiguous (VUCA) world, our people need to grow. Organizations globally are facing talent shortages because of aging populations. Our workforce is declining as Baby Boomers continue to retire more rapidly than Gen Z can enter the workforce. We cannot hire our way out of this talent shortage. We must develop expertise internally to meet our unique and growing staffing needs.

Ongoing rapid technological changes give rise to the need for new employee skills – those we know about, those we can anticipate, and skills that are currently unknown and will emerge. Organizations need to be resilient and adaptable to anticipate and respond quickly to technological changes and ensure their workforce has the necessary skills to meet new demands.

In response to today's stressors and tomorrow's demands, it's easy for leaders and organizations to fall into the trap of focusing on output above other priorities. While getting quarterly results, making sales quotes, or meeting production targets may achieve results in the short term, an output-focused workplace churns and burns great people. It's a short-term focus that eliminates the possibility of sustained growth for the future.

The alternative is developing people alongside achieving results. There needs to be flexibility in the workplace that allows time to learn and the opportunity to experiment and make mistakes without reprimand. Employees need to see a future for themselves that includes growing and learning new skills. Organizations need to be places where people grow. They need to provide more than a paycheque.

When organizations focus on learning, leaders nurture a Learning Mindset in themselves and role model it for their employees. They are curious and continually learning. They are courageous in their experiments, learning from mistakes, and comfortable with vulnerability. These leaders make learning part of who they are and how they show up. They lead with learning.

A leader's Learning Mindset extends to their team where they create a Team Culture of learning. Moving from an output-focused to a growth-focused workplace can be difficult and requires a sustained, committed effort from the leader to change. They need a vision for their team – they need to have a bias for growth that is not about the business but about the person, not about the results, but about their progress. To make the transition, leaders need to be uncomfortable with the status quo. How they are leading and how their team is functioning needs to be uncomfortable enough to be motivating.

Transitioning from output to growth through learning requires leaders to invest in their relationships with team members. Where perhaps they held a professional distance, they need to cultivate healthy, personal relationships with team members to build trust, connection, and commitment. The leader sheds their previous 'expert' or 'hero identity' and adopts a 'coaching identity' that prioritizes the employees' growth, learning, and success. This strengthens their relationship and increases the team's psychological safety.

In a workplace that prioritizes growth through learning, employees feel cared for and are engaged with work. They are committed to the leader, the team, and the organization, resulting in higher productivity and reduced turnover. The organization is developing leaders for tomorrow.

Finally, organizations that recognize how personal learning precedes performance and growth provide Organization Support. They are exceptionally clear that their expectation of leaders is to prioritize learning alongside results. They document and communicate these expectations, and the message aligns with the organization's culture. This congruence between what's said and what's done ensures leaders make room for coaching and developing their people. To support leaders, organizations provide resources. They celebrate leaders' successes, which rewards their coaching efforts and reinforces a broader culture of growth and learning.

When organizations and leaders focus on growth and embrace learning as the vehicle to achieve this growth, they create capacity for today and capability for tomorrow.

Too often, we sacrifice growth at the altar of results. We think it's about performance, accountability, and profit. But all of this comes after employee and team growth. By cultivating a Growth through Learning orientation, companies increase the capability of their employees. They build a workforce prepared for the future with all the demographic changes, skills shortages, and technology disruptions we will surely encounter. Learning moves out of a department and into the hands of leaders.

About the Author

Hannah is a passionate and engaging facilitator, author, and speaker who partners with leaders to develop exceptional employees for today, as well as employees who are prepared for the future. She does this by making learning central to their leadership and team culture. Drawing on more than 20 years of experience as a consultant, certified coach, and director of sales training, she is a recognized expert in leadership and team development.

Hannah holds a Masters in Adult Education and is a certified coach. She believes that work should be more than just a paycheque; it must be a place to learn and grow.

Work with me

These are some of the ways Hannah supports leaders in organizations:

- More than a Paycheque – Keynote focused on why learning needs to be central to an organization's employee engagement and growth strategy.

- Growth Academy – Program to help leaders coach and develop their employees for sustained growth. It includes a diagnostic, a personal report, and 1:1 coaching or workshops.
- Make Meetings Matter – Masterclass to embed continuous learning into team meetings and develop a Team Culture of learning so your people develop new skills and grow.
- Individual Career Development – For organizations without an established Learning and Development function, this program outlines employee learning and development paths that combine self-study, leader coaching, and Organization Support.

Hannah's other publications include:

- *Growth through Learning: Leadership Conversations for Employee Development* – A six-part podcast series based on this book. Listen to the leaders featured in these pages to hear their stories and experiences come to life.
- *Lead, Learn, Grow Conversation Cards* – A deck of question and action cards for team meetings and workshops. Take practical steps to nurture a Learning Mindset and foster a Team Culture of learning in your team and organization.
- *Training that Clicks: Virtual Design Playbook* – A how-to book for designing impactful virtual training courses that engage participants so they can actively apply what they learn.

Go to www.hannahbrown.co to learn more. You can also find Hannah on LinkedIn at www.linkedin.com/in/hannahbrown-learning/ to stay connected.

Gratitude

Thank you to all the leaders who generously gave their time to share their leadership journeys and perspectives on coaching and developing their teams. Many of your stories are reflected in this book, and some of you are featured in my podcast, *Growth through Learning: Leadership Conversations for Employee Development*. **All of you** helped shape the framework and my thinking for this book.

Adam Stephens

Andrew Ambrose

Andy Rombouts

Chantal McIntyre

Christy Billan

Christine Helgerman

Evelina Rog

Geoff Smith

Jason Leeder

Jerry Rice

Judy Bridges

Julianna Morris

Len Switzer

Lina Shamoun

Mark Harrison

Melissa Greer

Moira MacIntosh

Ola McAndrew

Patricia Hirst

Robin Young

Shaun Scott

Endnotes

PREFACE

1   OECD (2021). *Adult Learning and COVID-19: How much informal and non-formal learning are workers missing? OECD Policy Responses to Coronavirus (COVID-19)*, OECD Publishing: Paris. https://doi.org/10.1787/56a96569-e

2   Glassop, L. I. (2002). The organizational benefits of teams. *Human Relations, 55*(2), 225–249. https://doi.org/10.1177/001872670205500218

3   Edmondson, A. C. (2012). *Teaming: How Organizations Learn, Innovate, and Compete in the Knowledge Economy*. Hoboken, NJ: John Wiley & Sons.

CHAPTER 1

4   Ritchie, H., Rodés-Guirao, L., Mathieu, E., Gerber, M., Ortiz-Ospina, E., Hasell, J., & Roser, M. (2024, June 17). *Population growth*. Our World in Data. https://ourworldindata.org/population-growth?insight=population-growth-is-no-longer-exponential-it-peaked-decades-ago#key-insights

5   Government of Canada. (2022, April 27). *The Daily — In the midst of high job vacancies and historically low unemployment, Canada faces record retirements from an aging labour force: number of seniors aged 65 and older grows six times faster than children 0-14*. Statistics Canada. https://www150.statcan.gc.ca/n1/daily-quotidien/220427/dq220427a-eng.htm

6 Boatman, J., Neal, S., Rhyne, R., Watt, B., & Yeh, M (2023). *Global Leadership Forecast 2023*. Development Dimensions International (DDI). https://www.ddiworld.com/global-leadership-forecast-2023

7 Koetsier, J. (2022, April 21). *Self-Driving farm robot uses lasers to kill 100,000 weeds an hour, saving land and farmers from toxic herbicides*. Forbes. https://www.forbes.com/sites/johnkoetsier/2021/11/02/self-driving-farm-robot-uses-lasers-to-kill-100000-weeds-an-hour-saving-land-and-farmers-from-toxic-herbicides/

8 Hardman, P. (n.d). *How close is AI to replacing Instructional Designers: The Results Part 2: Selecting an Instructional Strategy*. LinkedIn. Retrieved August 5, 2024, from https://www.linkedin.com/posts/dr-philippa-hardman-057851120_ai-aied-instructionaldesign-activity-7225028574112559105-a9iB?utm_source=share&utm_medium=member_android

9 University of Waterloo. (n.d). *The Talent Evolution Series: The impact of AI on the future of work | Alumni*. Retrieved August 1, 2024, from https://uwaterloo.ca/alumni/events/talent-evolution-series-impact-ai-future-work

10 Korn Ferry. (2020). The Global Talent Crunch. In *Future of Work* (pp. 2–6). Korn Ferry. https://www.kornferry.com/content/dam/kornferry/docs/article-migration/FOWTalentCrunchFinal_Spring2018.pdf

11 Agrawal, S., De Smet, A., Poplawski, P., & Reich, A. (2020, February 12). *Beyond hiring: How companies are reskilling to address talent gaps*. McKinsey & Company. https://www.mckinsey.com/capabilities/people-and-organizational-performance/our-insights/beyond-hiring-how-companies-are-reskilling-to-address-talent-gaps

12 McKenna, J. (2023b, June 30). *Build a strong learning culture on your team*. Harvard Business Review. https://hbr.org/2023/06/build-a-strong-learning-culture-on-your-team

13 Wiles, J. (2021, December 09). *Great Resignation or Not, Money Won't Fix All Your Talent Problems*. Gartner. https://www.gartner.com/en/articles/great-resignation-or-not-money-won-t-fix-all-your-talent-problems

14 McKinsey & Company. (2023, August 2). *What is the gig economy?* McKinsey & Company. https://www.mckinsey.com/featured-insights/mckinsey-explainers/what-is-the-gig-economy

15   Plastino, E. (2022). *The Purpose Gap*. Cognizant. https://www.
      cognizant.com/en_us/insights/documents/the-purpose-gap-
      codex7086.pdf

16   Cook, I. (2021, September 15). *Who is driving the Great
      Resignation?* Harvard Business Review. https://hbr.org/2021/09/
      who-is-driving-the-great-resignation

17   Boatman, J., Neal, S., Rhyne, R., Watt, B., & Yeh, M
      (2023). *Global Leadership Forecast 2023*. Development
      Dimensions International (DDI). https://www.ddiworld.com/
      global-leadership-forecast-2023

18   Zenger, J., Folkman, J., & Folkman, Z. (2019). *How extraordinary
      leaders double profits*. Zenger Folkman. https://zengerfolkman.
      com/wp-content/uploads/2019/08/How-Extraordinary-Leaders-
      Double-Profit_WP-2019.pdf

19   Guggenberger, P., Maor, D., Park, M., & Simon, P. (2023). *The
      State of Organizations 2023: Ten shifts transforming organiza-
      tions* (Report). *McKinsey & Company*. https://www.mckinsey.
      com/capabilities/people-and-organizational-performance/
      our-insights/the-state-of-organizations-2023#/

20   Boatman, J., Neal, S., Rhyne, R., Watt, B., & Yeh, M
      (2023). *Global Leadership Forecast 2023*. Development
      Dimensions International (DDI). https://www.ddiworld.com/
      global-leadership-forecast-2023

21   Guggenberger, P., Maor, D., Park, M., & Simon, P. (2023). *The
      State of Organizations 2023: Ten shifts transforming organiza-
      tions* (Report). *McKinsey & Company*. https://www.mckinsey.
      com/capabilities/people-and-organizational-performance/
      our-insights/the-state-of-organizations-2023#/

22   Gallup (2024). *State of the Global Workplace Report*. Gallup Inc.
      https://www.gallup.com/workplace/349484/state-of-the-global-
      workplace.aspx

23   Guggenberger, P., Maor, D., Park, M., & Simon, P. (2023). *The
      State of Organizations 2023: Ten shifts transforming organiza-
      tions* (Report). *McKinsey & Company*. https://www.mckinsey.
      com/capabilities/people-and-organizational-performance/
      our-insights/the-state-of-organizations-2023#/

24   Herzberg, F. (1999). The Hygiene Motivation Theory. In *Thinkers
      101*. Chartered Management Institute.

25 World Economic Forum (WEF). (2021). *Future Readiness
    of SMEs Mobilizing the SME Sector to Drive Widespread
    Sustainability and Prosperity* (White paper). World Economic
    Forum. https://www3.weforum.org/docs/WEF_Future_
    Readiness_of_SMEs_2021.pdf

26 Gallup (2024). *State of the Global Workplace Report*. Gallup Inc.
    https://www.gallup.com/workplace/349484/state-of-the-global-
    workplace.aspx

27 Green, M. & Young, J. (2020). *Creating learning cultures: assess-
    ing the evidence* (Report, April 2020). Chartered Institute of
    Personnel and Development. https://www.cipd.org/globalassets/
    media/knowledge/knowledge-hub/reports/creating-learning-
    cultures-1_tcm18-75606.pdf

28 Madgavkar, A., Schaninger, B., Maor, D., White, O., Smit, S.,
    Samandari, H., Woetzel, L., Carlin, D., & Chockalingam, K. (2023).
    *Performance through people: Transforming human capital into
    competitive advantage. McKinsey & Company*. https://www.
    mckinsey.com/mgi/our-research/performance-through-people-
    transforming-human-capital-into-competitive-advantage

29 World Economic Forum (WEM). (2024, September 10).
    6 work and workplace trends to watch in 2024. World
    Economic Forum. https://www.weforum.org/agenda/2024/02/
    work-and-workplace-trends-to-watch-2024/

30 Zachosova, N., Kutsenko, D. & Koval, O. (2022). Strategy
    and Mechanism of Enterprises Financial and Economic
    Security Management in the conditions of war, industry 4.0
    and BANI world. *Financial and credit activity problems of
    theory and practice, 4*(45), 223-233. https://doi.org/10.55643/
    fcaptp.4.45.2022.3819.

31 *Future Impact – The Impact of AI and Technology.* (2023,
    February). Thought Leaders Business School Immersion.

32 Guggenberger, P., Maor, D., Park, M., & Simon, P. (2023). *The
    State of Organizations 2023: Ten shifts transforming organiza-
    tions* (Report). *McKinsey & Company*. https://www.mckinsey.
    com/capabilities/people-and-organizational-performance/
    our-insights/the-state-of-organizations-2023#/

33 Suarez, F., & Montes, J. (2020, November 1). *Building
    Organizational Resilience*. Harvard Business Review. https://hbr.
    org/2020/11/building-organizational-resilience

34 Gino, F. (2018, September – October). *The Business Case for Curiosity*. Harvard Business Review. https://hbr.org/2018/09/the-business-case-for-curiosity

35 Masden, P. & Desai, V. (2010). Failing to Learn? The Effects of Failure and Success on Organizational Learning in the Global Orbital Launch Vehicle Industry. *The Academy of Management Journal, 53*(3), 451–76. http://www.jstor.org/stable/2568433

36 Barrett, M. & Spencer, E. (2021, June 29). *Adaptability and Resilience: Lessons for Post-Pandemic Times*. American Management Association. https://www.amanet.org/articles/adaptability-and-resilience/

37 McKinsey & Company. (2020, October 5). *How COVID-19 has pushed companies over the technology tipping point—and transformed business forever*. McKinsey & Company. https://www.mckinsey.com/capabilities/strategy-and-corporate-finance/our-insights/how-covid-19-has-pushed-companies-over-the-technology-tipping-point-and-transformed-business-forever

38 Guggenberger, P., Maor, D., Park, M., & Simon, P. (2023). *The State of Organizations 2023: Ten shifts transforming organizations*. McKinsey & Company. https://www.mckinsey.com/capabilities/people-and-organizational-performance/our-insights/the-state-of-organizations-2023#/

39 Dethmer, J. Chapman, D. & Klemp, K. (2015). *The 15 Commitments of Conscious Leadership: A New Paradigm for Sustainable Success*. The Conscious Leadership Group.

40 Evenseth, L.L., Sydnes. M. & Gausdal, A.H. (2022). Building Organizational Resilience Through Organizational Learning: A Systematic Review. *Front. Commun, 7.* https://doi.org/10.3389/fcomm.2022.837386

41 Guggenberger, P., Maor, D., Park, M., & Simon, P. (2023). *The State of Organizations 2023: Ten shifts transforming organizations* (Report). *McKinsey & Company.* https://www.mckinsey.com/capabilities/people-and-organizational-performance/our-insights/the-state-of-organizations-2023#/

42 Ibid.

CHAPTER 2

43 Chapman, A. (Director). (2023). *Life on our Planet,* Season 1, Episode 7: Inheriting the Earth. Netflix. https://www.netflix.com/title/80213846,

44 Moar, D., Park, M., & Weddle, B. (2022, October 12). *Raising the resilience of your organization.* McKinsey & Company. https://www.mckinsey.com/capabilities/people-and-organizational-performance/our-insights/raising-the-resilience-of-your-organization#/

45 Kim, S., Lee, H., & Connerton, T. P. (2020). How Psychological safety Affects team performance: Mediating role of efficacy and learning behavior. *Frontiers in Psychology, 11.* https://doi.org/10.3389/fpsyg.2020.01581

46 Dyer, A., Puckett, S., Zhdan, S., Barybkina, E., & McManus. M. (2021, November 12). *Reach the Next Level by Learning How to Learn.* Boston Consulting Group. https://www.bcg.com/publications/2021/create-competitive-advantage-with-organizational-learning

47 Freifeld, L. (2023, November 14). *2023 Training Industry Report: Organizations kept a firm hand on training expenditures in 2022-2023, according to Training's Industry Report.* Training Magazine. https://trainingmag.com/2023-training-industry-report/

48 McKenna, J. (2006, June 6). *Build a Strong Learning Culture on Your Team.* Harvard Business Review. https://hbr.org/2023/06/build-a-strong-learning-culture-on-your-team

49 Ibid.

50 Kirkpatrick Partners, LLC. (2024, July 24). *What is The Kirkpatrick Model? / Kirkpatrick.* Accessed Oct 20, 2024. https://www.kirkpatrickpartners.com/the-kirkpatrick-model/

51 Carson, B. (2021). *L&D's Playbook for the Digital Age.* American Society for Training and Development.

CHAPTER 3

52 McKinsey Global Institute (2023). *Performance through people: Transforming human capital into competitive advantage* (Report). McKinsey & Company. https://www.mckinsey.com/mgi/our-research/performance-through-people-transforming-human-capital-into-competitive-advantage

53   Elnaga, A. & Imran, A. (2013). The Effect of Training on Employee Performance. *European Journal of Business and Management, 5*(4), 137-147. https://iiste.org/Journals/index.php/EJBM/article/view/4475

54   Han, Y., & Hong, S. (2019). The Impact of Accountability on Organizational Performance in the U.S. Federal Government: The Moderating Role of Autonomy. *Review of Public Personnel Administration, 39*(1), 3-23. https://doi.org/10.1177/0734371X16682816

55   Kelly, T. (2018). *Accountability and Employee Performance Case Study: Bambuiy Engineering Services & Techniques (B.E.S.T.) SARL*. Centria University of Applied Sciences. https://www.theseus.fi/bitstream/handle/10024/147663/Tsafack_%20Kelly.pdf?sequence=1

56   Green, M. & Young, J. (2020). *Creating learning cultures: assessing the evidence* (Report, April 2020). Chartered Institute of Personnel and Development. https://www.cipd.org/globalassets/media/knowledge/knowledge-hub/reports/creating-learning-cultures-1_tcm18-75606.pdf

CHAPTER 4

57   Vandewalle, D., Brown, S., Cron, W. & Slocum, J. (1999). The Influence of Goal Orientation and Self-Regulation Tactics on Sales Performance: A Longitudinal Field Test. *Journal of Applied Psychology, 84*. 249-259. https://doi.org/10.1037/0021-9010.84.2.249

58   FourWeekMBA (n.d). *The Leading Source of Insights On Business Model Strategy & Tech Business Models*. Four Week MBA. Retrieved June 30, 2024. from https://fourweekmba.com/tesla-vision-statement-mission-statement/

59   Llewellyn-Jones, J. (Director) (2022). *The Elon Musk Show*. Episode 2. Retrieved February 13, 2024 from https://www.bbc.co.uk/iplayer/episodes/m001d1n9/the-elon-musk-show

60   Hawkins, A. (2023, August 16). *Tesla's 'ultra hardcore' work culture — as told by its employees*. The Verge. https://www.theverge.com/2023/8/16/23833447/tesla-elon-musk-ultra-hardcore-employees-land-of-the-giants

61   Reed, E. & Diongson, D. (2024, April 30). *History of Tesla & its stock: Timeline, facts & milestones.* The Street. https://www.thestreet.com/technology/history-of-tesla-15088992

62   Cardenas, B. (2021, September 13). *Tesla Case Study: Complete Assessment of Social/Organizational Culture, Leadership, Teams, Communication, Talent/Knowledge Management & Recommendations.* LinkedIn. https://www.linkedin.com/pulse/tesla-case-study-complete-assessment-culture-teams-bianca/

63   Ohnsman, A. (2019, April 30). *Inside Tesla's Model 3 Factory, Where Safety Violations Keep Rising.* Forbes. https://www.forbes.com/sites/alanohnsman/2019/03/01/tesla-safety-violations-dwarf-big-us-auto-plants-in-aftermath-of-musks-model-3-push/?sh=13255cb454ce

64   O'Kane, S. (2020, January 29). *Tesla's recorded 2019 has brought it some breathing room: Back-to-back quarterly profits to finish the year.* The Verge. https://www.theverge.com/2020/1/29/21113987/tesla-q4-2019-earnings-results-profit-revenue-model-3.

65   Ibid.

66   Zandt, F. (2024, January 25). *How Successful is Tesla?* Statista. https://www.statista.com/chart/26705/yearly-net-income-and-revenue-of-tesla/

67   Ibid

68   Cardenas, B. (2021, September 13). *Tesla Case Study: Complete Assessment of Social/Organizational Culture, Leadership, Teams, Communication, Talent/Knowledge Management & Recommendations.* LinkedIn. https://www.linkedin.com/pulse/tesla-case-study-complete-assessment-culture-teams-bianca/

69   Diaz, J. (2023. January 24). *How Tesla's design took it from innovator to dud: The electrical vehicle boom is bad news for Tesla.* Fast Company. https://www.fastcompany.com/90833755/how-teslas-design-took-it-from-innovator-to-dud

70   Rapier, R. (2022, December 19). *Why Tesla's Market Share Is Set To Plunge In 2023.* Fast Company. https://www.forbes.com/sites/rrapier/2022/12/19/why-teslas-market-share-could-plunge-in-2023/?sh=620c6de4439d

71   Diaz, J. (2023. January 24). *How Tesla's design took it from innovator to dud: The electrical vehicle boom is bad news for Tesla.* Fast Company. https://www.fastcompany.com/90833755/how-teslas-design-took-it-from-innovator-to-dud

72   Ibid.

CHAPTER 5

73   Pink, D. (2009). *Drive: The Surprising Truth About What Motivates Us.* Penguin Books.

74   Moss, J. (2021). *The Burnout Epidemic: The Rise of Chronic Stress and How We Can Fix It.* Harvard Business Review Press.

75   Alo, O., Arslan, A., Tian, A.Y. & Pereira, V. (2023). Exploring the limits of mindfulness during the COVID-19 pandemic: Qualitative evidence from African context. *Journal of Managerial Psychology, 39*(3), 372-402. https://doi.org/10.1108/JMP-03-2022-0124.

76   Monahan, K., Cotteleer, M. J. & Fisher, J. (2016). *Does scarcity make you dumb? A behavioral understanding of how scarcity diminishes our decision making and control.* Deloitte University Press.

77   Ibid.

78   McKinsey Global Institute (2023). *Performance through people: Transforming human capital into competitive advantage* (Report). McKinsey & Company. https://www.mckinsey.com/mgi/our-research/performance-through-people-transforming-human-capital-into-competitive-advantage

CHAPTER 6

79   Based on work completed by the author at Benchmark Performance Inc. and the work of David E. Wiley:

Wiley, D. E. (2014). Why Doers Do – Part 1: Internal Elements of Human Performance. *Performance Improvement, 53*(2), 14-20.

Wiley, D. E. (2014). Why Doers Do – Part 2: External-Tangible Elements of Human Performance. *Performance Improvement, 53*(3), 5-13.

Wiley, D. E. (2014) Why Doers Do – Part 3: External-Intangible Elements of Human Performance. *Performance Improvement, 53*(4). 6-14.

80   Kelly, T. (2018). *Accountability and Employee Performance Case Study: Bambuiy Engineering Services & Techniques (B.E.S.T.) SARL*. Centria University of Applied Sciences. https://www.theseus.fi/bitstream/handle/10024/147663/Tsafack_%20Kelly.pdf?sequence=1

81   Chang, CH., Shao, R., Wang, M. & Baker, N.M. (2021). Workplace Interventions in Response to COVID-19: an Occupational Health Psychology Perspective, *Occupational Health Science, 5*, 1–23. https://doi.org/10.1007/s41542-021-00080-x

82   Bresman, H. and Edmondson, A. (2022, March 17). *Research To Excel, Diverse Teams Needs Psychological Safety: Findings from a study of 62 drug-development teams*. Harvard Business Review. https://hbr.org/2022/03/research-to-excel-diverse-teams-need-psychological-safety

83   Ryan, R. & Deci, E. (2000). Self-Determination Theory and the Facilitation of Intrinsic Motivation, Social Development, and Well-Being. *American Psychologist, 55*(1), 68-78.

84   Pink, D. (2009). *Drive: The Surprising Truth About What Motivates Us*. Penguin Books.

85   Kalchman, L. (2003, January 25). *Making NHL a very long shot*. Hockey Canada Foundation. https://www.hockeycanada.ca/en-ca/news/2003-gn-001-en

86   Gallup (2024). *State of the Global Workplace Report*. Gallup Inc. https://www.gallup.com/workplace/349484/state-of-the-global-workplace.aspx

87   Rowley, M. (2020, August 2). *Why Stress is a Workplace Safety Issue*. Columbia Southern University. https://www.columbiasouthern.edu/blog/blog-articles/2020/august/stress-and-safety-in-the-workplace/

88   Achor, S. (2011). The happiness advantage: the seven principles of positive psychology that fuel success and performance at work. *Choice Reviews Online, 48*(07), 48–4166. https://doi.org/10.5860/choice.48-4166

89   Masden, P.M. & Desai, V. (2010). Failing to Learn? The Effects of Failure and Success on Organizational Learning in the Global Orbital Launch Vehicle Industry. *The Academy of Management Journal, 53* (3),451–76. http://www.jstor.org/stable/25684332

90 Navarra, K. (2022, April 11). *The Real Costs of Recruitment.*
    Society for Human Resource Management (SHRM). https://
    www.shrm.org/topics-tools/news/talent-acquisition/
    real-costs-recruitment

CHAPTER 7

91 Dekker, T. (2023, June 15). *How businesses can stand the test of
    time.* Ernst & Young Global Ltd (EY). https://www.ey.com/en_gl/
    insights/consulting/how-businesses-can-stand-the-test-of-time

92 Shepherd, C. (2015). *More than Blended Learning: Designing
    world-class learning interventions.* Eastleigh UK: The More Than
    Blended Learning Company.

CHAPTER 8

93 Bridges, W. (2004). *Transitions: Making Sense of Life's Changes.*
    Da Capo Press.

CHAPTER 9

94 Dweck, C. (2007). *Mindset: The New Psychology of Success.*
    Ballantine Books.

95 Leslie, I. (2014). *Curious: The Desire to Know and Why Your
    Future Depends on it.* Basic Books.

96 Gino, F. (2018, September – October). *The Business Case for
    Curiosity.* Harvard Business Review. https://hbr.org/2018/09/
    the-business-case-for-curiosity

97 Ibid.

98 Ibid.

99 Ibid.

100 Chamorro-Premuzic, T. (2023, November 3). *How to Strengthen
    your Curiosity Muscle.* Harvard Business Review. https://hbr.
    org/2023/11/how-to-strengthen-your-curiosity-muscle

101 Gino, F. (2018, September – October). *The Business Case for
    Curiosity.* Harvard Business Review. https://hbr.org/2018/09/
    the-business-case-for-curiosity

102 Gruber, M.J., Gelman, B.D., & Ranganath, C (2014). States of
     Curiosity Modulate Hippocampus-Dependent Learning via
     the Dopaminergic Circuit. *Neuron*, 84(2), 486–496. http://doi.
     org/10.1016/j.neuron.2014.08.060

103 Jirout, J., Vitiello, V. & Zumbrunn, S. (2018). Curiosity
     in Schools. In The New Science of Curiosity. Nova
     Science Publishers. https://www.researchgate.net/
     publication/329569586_CURIOSITY_IN_SCHOOLS

104 Gino, F. (2018, September – October). *The Business Case for
     Curiosity*. Harvard Business Review. https://hbr.org/2018/09/
     the-business-case-for-curiosity

105 Future of jobs 2023: These are the most in-demand skills now -
     and beyond. World Economic Forum, May 1, 2023. https://www.
     weforum.org/agenda/2023/05/future-of-jobs-2023-skills/

106 Gino, F. (2018, September – October). *The Business Case for
     Curiosity*. Harvard Business Review. https://hbr.org/2018/09/
     the-business-case-for-curiosity

107 Ibid.

108 Leslie, I. (2014). *Curious: The Desire to Know and Why Your
     Future Depends on it*. Basic Books.

109 Gino, F. (2018, September – October). *The Business Case for
     Curiosity*. Harvard Business Review. https://hbr.org/2018/09/
     the-business-case-for-curiosity

110 Leslie, I. (2014). *Curious: The Desire to Know and Why Your
     Future Depends on it*. Basic Books.

111 Gino, F. (2018, September – October). *The Business Case for
     Curiosity*. Harvard Business Review. https://hbr.org/2018/09/
     the-business-case-for-curiosity

112 Leslie, I. (2014). *Curious: The Desire to Know and Why Your
     Future Depends on it*. Basic Books.

113 Draganski, B., Gaser, C., Kempermann, G., Kuhn, H. G., Winkler, J.,
     Büchel, C., & May, A. (2006). Temporal and spatial dynamics of
     brain structure changes during extensive learning. *The Journal
     of Neuroscience, 26*(23), 6314-6317. https://doi.org/10.1523/
     JNEUROSCI.4628-05.200

114 Maguire, E. A., Gadian, D. G., Johnsrude, I. S., Good, C. D., Ashburner, J., Frackowiak, R. S., & Frith, C. D. (2000). Navigation-related structural change in the hippocampi of taxi drivers. *Proceedings of the National Academy of Sciences of the United States of America, 97*(8), 4398–4403. https://doi.org/10.1073/pnas.07003959

115 Edmondson, A.C. & Bransby, D.P. (2023). Psychological Safety Comes of Age: Observed Themes in an Established Literature. *Annual Review of Organizational Psychology & Organizational Behavior, 10*(1), 55-78. http://dx.doi.org/10.1146/annurev-orgpsych-120920-055217

116 Schein, E.H. (1965). *Personal and Organizational Change through Group Methods: The Laboratory Approach.* New York: Wiley

117 Schein E.H. (1993, January 15). *How can organizations learn faster? The challenge of entering the green room.* MIT Sloan Management Review Magazine. https://sloanreview.mit.edu/article/how-can-organizations-learn-faster-the-challenge-of-entering-the-green-room/

118 Edmondson, A.C. & Bransby, D.P. (2023). Psychological Safety Comes of Age: Observed Themes in an Established Literature. *Annual Review of Organizational Psychology & Organizational Behavior, 10*(1), 55-78. http://dx.doi.org/10.1146/annurev-orgpsych-120920-055217

119 Ibid.

120 Edmondson, A. (2018). *Creating Psychological Safety in the Workplace for Learning, Innovation, and Growth.* Wiley.

121 Edmondson, A.C. & Bransby, D.P. (2023). Psychological Safety Comes of Age: Observed Themes in an Established Literature. *Annual Review of Organizational Psychology & Organizational Behavior, 10*(1), 55-78. http://dx.doi.org/10.1146/annurev-orgpsych-120920-055217

122 Castro D.R., Anseel, F., Kluger, A.N., Lloyd, K.J., & Turjeman-Levi, Y. (2018). Mere listening effect on creativity and the mediating role of psychological safety. *Psychology of Aesthetics, Creativity, and the Arts, 12*(4), 489–502. https://doi.org/10.1037/aca0000177

123 Mao, J., Chiang, J.T., Chen, L., Wu, Y., & Wang, J. (2019). Feeling safe? A conservation of resources perspective examining the interactive effect of leader competence and leader self-serving behaviour on team performance. *Journal of Occupational and Organizational Psychology, 92*(1), 52–73. https://doi.org/10.1111/joop.12233

124 Han, Y., Hao, P., Yang, B., & Liu, W. (2017). How leaders' transparent behavior influences employee creativity: The mediating roles of psychological safety and ability to focus attention. *Journal of Leadership and Organizational Studies, 24*(3), 335–44. https://doi.org/10.1177/1548051816670306

125 Weisul, K. & Maclean, A. (2013, September 26). *4 Powerful Things Leaders Should Know About Vulnerability*. Inc.com. https://www.inc.com/kimberly-weisul-and-andrew-maclean/dr-brene-brown-vulnerability-leadership.html

126 Boatman, J., Neal, S., Rhyne, R., Watt, B., & Yeh, M (2023). *Global Leadership Forecast 2023*. Development Dimensions International (DDI). https://www.ddiworld.com/global-leadership-forecast-2023

127 Ibid.

128 Ibid.

129 Wilson, R. S., Boyle, P. A., Yu, L., Segawa, E., Sytsma, J., & Bennett, D. A. (2015). Conscientiousness, dementia related pathology, and trajectories of cognitive aging. Psychology and Aging, 30(1), 74–82. https://doi.org/10.1037/pag0000013

130 Edmondson, A.C. & Bransby, D.P. (2023). Psychological Safety Comes of Age: Observed Themes in an Established Literature. *Annual Review of Organizational Psychology & Organizational Behavior, 10*(1), 55-78. http://dx.doi.org/10.1146/annurev-orgpsych-120920-055217

131 Edmondson, A. (2018). *The Fearless Organization: Creating Psychological Safety in the Workplace for Learning, Innovation, and Growth.* Wiley.

132 Gibbs, R. (2020, July 5). *Four Positive Effects Of Fostering A Learning Organization*. Forbes Coaches Council. https://www.forbes.com/councils/forbescoachescouncil/2020/06/05/four-positive-effects-of-fostering-a-learning-organization/

133 Duhigg, C. (2014). *The Power of Habit: Why we do what we do in life and business.* Anchor Canada.

134 Clear. J. (2018). *Atomic Habits: An Easy & Proven Way to Build Good Habits & Break Bad Ones.* Avery.

CHAPTER 10

135 Merriam-Webster. (n.d). Culture. Retrieved July 14, 2024, from https://www.merriam-webster.com/dictionary/culture

136 Gallup (2024, July 14). *What Is Organizational Culture? And Why Does It Matter?* Gallup Inc. https://www.gallup.com/workplace/327371/how-to-build-better-company-culture.asp

137 Coyle, D. (2018). *Secrets of Highly Successful Groups.* Random House Business Books.

138 Dethmer, J. Chapman, D. & Klemp, K. (2015). *The 15 Commitments of Conscious Leadership: A New Paradigm for Sustainable Success.* The Conscious Leadership Group.

139 Integral Coaching Canada. https://www.integralcoachingcanada.com/

140 Matt Church is the founder of the Thought Leaders Business School. https://thoughtleaders.com.au/

141 Schein, E. & Schein, P. (n.d.). Episode 539: The Path Towards Trusting Relationships. *Coaching for Leaders Podcast.* Retrieved July 11, 2024, from https://coachingforleaders.com/podcast/trusting-relationships-edgar-schein-peter-schein/

142 Schein, E. and Schein, P. (2021). *Humble Inquiry, Second Edition: The Gentle Art of Asking Instead of Telling.* Berrett-Koehler Publishers.

143 Duncan, D. (2018, November 19). *Want To Increase Your Leadership Effectiveness? Be Humble.* Forbes. https://www.forbes.com/sites/rodgerdeanduncan/2018/11/19/want-to-increase-your-leadership-effectiveness-be-humble/

144 Salovey, P. & Mayer, J.D. (1990). Emotional intelligence. *Imagination, Cognition and Personality.* 9(3), 185–211. https://doi.org/10.2190/DUGG-P24E-52WK-6CDG

145 Mayer, J.D. (1997). Salovey what is emotional intelligence? In: Salovey, P. & Sluyter, D.J. (Eds.) (1997). *Emotional Development and Emotional Intelligence: Implications for Educators* (pp. 3–31). Basic Books.

146 Goleman, D. (1995). *Emotional Intelligence: Why It Can Matter More Than IQ.* Random House Publishing Group.

147 Abraham, R. (1999). Emotional intelligence in organizations: a conceptualization *Genetic, Social, and General Psychology Monographs, 125* (2), 209–224. https://www.sciepub.com/reference/87367

148 Thoits, P.A. (1989). The sociology of emotions. *Annual Review of Sociology, 15,* 317–342. https://doi.org/10.1146/annurev.so.15.080189.001533

149 Scott, S. G., & Bruce, R. A. (1994). Determinants of innovative behavior: A path model of individual innovation in the workplace. *Academy of Management Journal, 37*(3), 580–607. https://doi.org/10.2307/256701

150 Raetze, S., Duchek, S., Maynard, M. T., & Wohlgemuth, M. (2022). Resilience in organization-related research: An integrative conceptual review across disciplines and levels of analysis. *Journal of Applied Psychology, 107*(6), 867–897. https://doi.org/10.1037/apl0000952

151 Boyatzis, R.E. (1982). *The Competent Manager: A Model for Effective Performance.* Wiley.

152 Petrides, K. V., Furnham, A., & Mavroveli, S. (2007). Trait emotional intelligence: Moving forward in the field of EI. In G. Matthews, M. Zeidner, & R. D. Roberts (Eds.), *The science of emotional intelligence: Knowns and unknowns* (pp. 151–166). Oxford University Press.

153 Goleman, D. (1998). *Working with Emotional Intelligence.* Bantam Publishing.

Also

Alo, O., Arslan, A., Tian, A.Y. & Pereira, V. (2023). Exploring the limits of mindfulness during the COVID-19 pandemic: Qualitative evidence from African context. *Journal of Managerial Psychology.* https://doi.org/10.1108/JMP-03-2022-0124.

154 Gabriel, Y & Griffiths, D.S. (2002). Emotion, learning and organizing. *The Learning Organization, 9,* 214–221. https://doi.org/10.1108/09696470210442169

155 Rosete D. & Ciarrochi, J. (2005). Emotional intelligence and its relationship to workplace performance outcomes of leadership effectiveness. *The Leadership Organization, 26,* 388–399. https://doi.org/10.1108/01437730510607871

156 Hogan, D. & Shelton, A. (1998). A socioanalytic perspective on job performance, *Human Performance, 11*(2), 129–144, https//doi.org/10.1207/s15327043hup1102&3_2

157 Riggio, R. E., & Reichard, R. J. (2008). The emotional and social intelligences of effective leadership: An emotional and social skill approach. *Journal of Managerial Psychology, 23*(2), 169–185. https://doi.org/10.1108/02683940810850808

158 Rafaeli, A. & Worline, M. (2001). Individual emotion in work organizations. *Social Science Information, 40,* 95–123.

159 Coronado-Maldonado, I. & Benítez-Márquez, M.D. (2023). Emotional intelligence, leadership, and work teams: A hybrid literature review. *Heliyon, 9*(10). https//doi.org/10.1016/j.heliyon.2023.e20356

160 Barsade, S.G. & Gibson, D.E. (1998). Group emotion: A view from top and bottom. In: Gruenfeld, D.H. (Ed.), Research on Managing Groups and Teams, Elsevier Science/JAI Press Inc.(pp. 81–102). https://www.researchgate.net/profile/Sigal-Barsade/publication/284024690_Group_emotion_A_view_from_top_and_bottom/links/56e2140e08ae4e3e9428223a/Group-emotion-A-view-from-top-and-bottom.pdf

161 Clarke, N. (2010). Emotional intelligence and its relationship to transformational leadership and key project manager competences. *Project Management Journal, 41,* 5–20.

162 Ibid.

163 Jung, H.S. & Yoon, H.H. (2019). Emotional contagion and collective commitment among leaders and team members in deluxe hotel. *Service Business, 13,* 737–754.

164 Liu, X. & Liu, J. (2013). Effects of team leader emotional intelligence and team emotional climate on team member job satisfaction: a cross-level. *Nankai Business Review International, 4,* 180–198.

165 Gavin, D.J., Gavin, J.H. & Quick, J.C. (2017). Power struggles within the top management team: an empirical examination of follower reactions to subversive leadership. *Journal of Applied Biobehavioral Research, 22,* 1–15. https://doi.org/10.1111/jabr.12100

166 Martinko, M.J., Harvey, P., Brees, J.R. & Mackey, J. (2013). *A review of abusive supervision research, Journal of Organizational Behaviour, 34,*120–137.

167 Dasborough, M.T., Ashkanasy, N.M., Humphrey, R.H. Harms, P.D., Cred´e, M. & Wood, D. (2022). Does leadership still not need emotional intelligence? Continuing "The Great EI Debate", *Leadership Quarterly, 33.*

168 Bungay Stanier, M. (2016). *The Coaching Habit: Say Less, Ask More & Change the Way You Lead Forever.* Box of Crayons Press.

CHAPTER 11

169 Smith, M & Young McNally, E. (2021, April 16). The McKinsey & Company podcast: Building a learning culture that drives business forward. Retrieved August 18, 2024, from https://www.mckinsey.com/capabilities/ people-and-organizational-performance/our-insights/ building-a-learning-culture-that-drives-business-forward

170 Bersin by Deloitte (n.d.). Infographic: Leading in Learning: Building capabilities to deliver on your business strategy. Retrieved August 18, 2024. https://www2.deloitte.com/content/ dam/Deloitte/global/Documents/HumanCapital/gx-cons-hc-learning-solutions-placemat.pdf

171 McKenna, J. (2023, June 30). *Build a strong learning culture on your team.* Harvard Business Review. https://hbr.org/2023/06/ build-a-strong-learning-culture-on-your-team

172 Gallup (2024, March 20). *Why the Onboarding Experience Is Key for Retention.* Gallup Inc. https://www.gallup.com/work-place/235121/why-onboarding-experience-key-retention.aspx

173 Hirsch, A. S. (2023, December 21). *Don't underesti-mate the importance of good onboarding.* The Society for Human Resource Management (*SHRM*). https:// www.shrm.org/topics-tools/news/talent-acquisition/ dont-underestimate-importance-good-onboarding

174 Kantor, J. S. (2017, February 11). *High turnover costs way more than you think.* HuffPost. https://www.huffpost.com/entry/ high-turnover-costs-way-more-than-you-think_b_9197238?utm_ source=link_wwwv9&utm_campaign=item_235121&utm_ medium=copy

175   Boatman, J., Neal, S., Rhyne, R., Watt, B., & Yeh, M
       (2023). *Global Leadership Forecast 2023*. Development
       Dimensions International (DDI). https://www.ddiworld.com/
       global-leadership-forecast-2023

176   McKinsey Global Institute (2021, July 1). *The social economy:
       Unlocking value and productivity through social technologies*.
       McKinsey & Company. https://www.mckinsey.com/industries/
       technology-media-and-telecommunications/our-insights/
       the-social-economy

177   Gallup & Work Human (2023, March 29). *From Praise
       to Profits: The Business Case for Recognition at Work*.
       Work Human. Retrieved July 24, 2024 from https://
       www.workhuman.com/resources/reports-guides/
       from-praise-to-profits-workhuman-gallup-report/

178   Ibid.

179   Ibid.

180   Ibid.

CHAPTER 12

181   Corporate English Solutions (2023, February 26). *How L&D can
       positively impact workplace well-being*. British Council. Retrieved
       August 20, 2024, from https://corporate.britishcouncil.org/
       insights/how-ld-can-positively-impact-workplace-well-being

CHAPTER 13

182   Edmondson, A (2023). *Right Kind of Wrong: The Science of
       Failing Well*. New York, NY: Atria Books.

CHAPTER 14

183   Corporate English Solutions (2023, January 30). *5 ways
       L&D is crucial for talent retention*. British Council. Retrieved
       August 20, 2024 from https://corporate.britishcouncil.org/
       insights/5-ways-ld-crucial-talent-retention

184   Green, M. & Young, J. (2020). *Creating learning cultures: assessing the evidence* (Report, April 2020). Chartered Institute of Personnel and Development. https://www.cipd.org/globalassets/media/knowledge/knowledge-hub/reports/creating-learning-cultures-1_tcm18-75606.pdf

185   Maunder, R. G., Heeney, N. D., Strudwick, G., Shin, H. D., O'Neill, B., Young, N., Jeffs, L. P., Barrett, K., Bodmer, N. S., Born, K. B., Hopkins, J., Jüni, P., Perkhun, A., Price, D. J., Razak, F., Mushquash, C. J., & Mah, L. (2021). *Burnout in Hospital-Based Healthcare Workers during COVID-19. Science Advisory Table, 1.* https://doi.org/10.47326/ocsat.2021.02.46.1.0

186   Government of Canada (2022, June 3). *The Daily — Experiences of health care workers during the COVID-19 pandemic, September to November 2021.* Statistics Canada. https://www150.statcan.gc.ca/n1/daily-quotidien/220603/dq220603a-eng.htm

187   Mehta, S. (2024, March 6). *Satya Nadella's 3-word description of Microsoft's culture should inspire leaders to be learners.* Fast Company. https://www.fastcompany.com/91133383/microsoft-ceo-satya-nadella-3-word-description-microsoft-culture-leadership

.

www.ingramcontent.com/pod-product-compliance
Lightning Source LLC
Chambersburg PA
CBHW040918210326
41597CB00030B/5113